Streaming Architecture
New Designs Using Apache Kafka and MapR Streams

Ted Dunning and Ellen Friedman

Beijing · Boston · Farnham · Sebastopol · Tokyo

Streaming Architecture

by Ted Dunning and Ellen Friedman

Printed in the United States of America.

Published by O'Reilly Media, Inc., 1005 Gravenstein Highway North, Sebastopol, CA 95472.

O'Reilly books may be purchased for educational, business, or sales promotional use. Online editions are also available for most titles (*http://safaribooksonline.com*). For more information, contact our corporate/institutional sales department: 800-998-9938 or *corporate@oreilly.com*.

Editors: Holly Bauer and Nicole Tache   **Cover Designer:** Randy Comer

March 2016:   First Edition

Revision History for the First Edition
2016-03-07:   First Release
2016-05-09:   Second Release

978-1-491-95392-1

[LSI]

Table of Contents

Preface

The ability to handle and process continuous streams of data provides a considerable competitive edge. As a result, being able to take advantage of streaming data is beginning to be seen as an essential part of building a data-driven organization.

The expanding use of streaming data raises the question of how best to design systems to handle it effectively, from the ingestion from multiple sources, through a variety of uses, including streaming analytics and the question of persistence.

Emerging best practices for the design of streaming architectures may surprise you—the scope of powerful design for streaming systems extends far beyond specific real-time or near–real time applications. New approaches to streaming designs can greatly improve the efficiency of your overall organization.

Who Should Use This Book

If you already use streaming data and want to design an architecture for best performance, or if you are just starting to explore the value of streaming data, this book should be helpful. You'll also find real-world use cases that help you see how to put these approaches to work in several different settings. For developers, you'll also find links to sample programs.

This book is designed for both nontechnical and technical audiences, including business analysts, architects, team leaders, data scientists, and developers.

What Is Covered

In this book, we:

- Explain how to recognize opportunities where streaming data may be useful
- Show how to design streaming architecture for best results in a multiuser system
- Describe why particular capabilities should be present in the message-passing layer to take advantage of this type of design
- Explain why stream-based architectures are helpful to support microservices
- Describe particular tools for messaging and streaming analytics that best fit the requirements of a strong stream-based design.

Chapters 1–3 explain the basic aspects of strong architecture for streaming and microservices. If you are already familiar with many business goals for streaming data, you may want to start with Chapter 2, in which we describe the type of architecture that we recommend for streaming systems.

In addition to explaining the capabilities needed to support this emerging best practice, we also describe some of the currently available technologies that meet these requirements well. Chapter 4 goes into some detail on Apache Kafka, including links to sample programs provided by the authors. Chapter 5 describes another preferred technology for effective message passing known as MapR Streams, which uses the Apache Kafka API but with some additional capabilities.

Later chapters provide a deeper dive into real-world use cases that employ streaming data as well as a look forward to how this exciting field is likely to evolve.

Conventions Used in This Book

The following typographical conventions are used in this book:

Italic
: Indicates new terms, URLs, email addresses, filenames, and file extensions.

Constant width

> Used for program listings, as well as within paragraphs to refer to program elements such as variable or function names, databases, data types, environment variables, statements, and keywords.

 This icon indicates a general note.

 This icon signifies a tip or suggestion.

 This icon indicates a warning or caution.

Supplemental material (code examples, exercises, etc.) is available for download at: *https://www.mapr.com/blog/getting-started-sample-programs-apache-kafka-09* and *https://www.mapr.com/blog/getting-started-sample-programs-mapr-streams*

This book is here to help you get your job done. In general, if example code is offered with this book, you may use it in your programs and documentation. You do not need to contact us for permission unless you're reproducing a significant portion of the code. For example, writing a program that uses several chunks of code from this book does not require permission. Selling or distributing a CD-ROM of examples from O'Reilly books does require permission. Answering a question by citing this book and quoting example code does not require permission. Incorporating a significant amount of example code from this book into your product's documentation does require permission.

We appreciate, but do not require, attribution. An attribution usually includes the title, author, publisher, and ISBN. For example: "*Streaming Architecture* by Ted Dunning and Ellen Friedman

(O'Reilly). Copyright 2016 Ted Dunning and Ellen Friedman, 978-1-491-95392-1."

If you feel your use of code examples falls outside fair use or the permission given above, feel free to contact us at *permissions@oreilly.com*.

Safari® Books Online

 *Safari Books Online* is an on-demand digital library that delivers expert content in both book and video form from the world's leading authors in technology and business.

Technology professionals, software developers, web designers, and business and creative professionals use Safari Books Online as their primary resource for research, problem solving, learning, and certification training.

Safari Books Online offers a range of plans and pricing for enterprise, government, education, and individuals.

Members have access to thousands of books, training videos, and prepublication manuscripts in one fully searchable database from publishers like O'Reilly Media, Prentice Hall Professional, Addison-Wesley Professional, Microsoft Press, Sams, Que, Peachpit Press, Focal Press, Cisco Press, John Wiley & Sons, Syngress, Morgan Kaufmann, IBM Redbooks, Packt, Adobe Press, FT Press, Apress, Manning, New Riders, McGraw-Hill, Jones & Bartlett, Course Technology, and hundreds more. For more information about Safari Books Online, please visit us online.

How to Contact Us

Please address comments and questions concerning this book to the publisher:

O'Reilly Media, Inc.
1005 Gravenstein Highway North
Sebastopol, CA 95472
800-998-9938 (in the United States or Canada)
707-829-0515 (international or local)

707-829-0104 (fax)

We have a web page for this book, where we list errata, examples, and any additional information. You can access this page at *http://bit.ly/streaming-architecture*.

To comment or ask technical questions about this book, send email to *bookquestions@oreilly.com*.

For more information about our books, courses, conferences, and news, see our website at *http://www.oreilly.com*.

Find us on Facebook: *http://facebook.com/oreilly*

Follow us on Twitter: *http://twitter.com/oreillymedia*

Watch us on YouTube: *http://www.youtube.com/oreillymedia*

CHAPTER 1

Why Stream?

Life doesn't happen in batches.

Many of the systems we want to monitor and to understand happen as a continuous stream of events—heartbeats, ocean currents, machine metrics, GPS signals. The list, like the events, is essentially endless. It's natural, then, to want to collect and analyze information from these events as a stream of data. Even analysis of sporadic events such as website traffic can benefit from a streaming data approach.

There are many potential advantages of handling data as streams, but until recently this method was somewhat difficult to do well. Streaming data and real-time analytics formed a fairly specialized undertaking rather than a widespread approach. *Why, then, is there now an explosion of interest in streaming?*

The short answer to that question is that superb new technologies are now available to handle streaming data at high-performance levels and at large scale—and that is leading more organizations to handle data as a stream. The improvements in these technologies are not subtle. Extremely high performance at scale is one of the chief advances, though not the only one. Previous rates of message throughput for persistent message queues were in the range of thousands of messages per second. The new technologies we discuss in this book can deliver rates of millions of messages per second, even while persisting the messages. These systems can be scaled horizontally to achieve even higher rates, and improved performance at scale isn't the only benefit you can get from modern streaming systems.

The upshot of these changes is that getting real-time insights from streaming data has gone from promise to widespread practice. As it turns out, stream-based architectures additionally provide fundamental and powerful benefits.

 Streaming data is not just for highly specialized projects. Stream-based computing is becoming the norm for data-driven organizations.

New technologies and architectural designs let you build flexible systems that are not only more efficient and easier to build, but that also better model the way business processes take place. This is true in part because the new systems decouple dependencies between processes that deliver data and processes that make use of data. Data from many sources can be streamed into a modern data platform and used by a variety of consumers almost immediately or at a later time as needed. The possibilities are intriguing.

We will explain why this broader view of streaming architecture is valuable, but first we take a look at how people use streaming data, now or in the very near future. One of the foremost sources of continuous data is from sensors in the Internet of Things (IoT), and a rapidly evolving sector in IoT is the development of futuristic "connected vehicles."

Planes, Trains, and Automobiles: Connected Vehicles and the IoT

In the case of the modern and near-future personal automobile, it will likely be exchanging information with several different audiences. These may include the driver, the manufacturer, the telematics provider, in some cases the insurance company, the car itself, and soon, other cars on the road.

Connected cars are one of the fastest-changing specialties in the IoT connected vehicles arena, but the idea is not entirely new. One of the earliest connected vehicles—a distant harbinger of today's designs— came to the public's attention in the early 1970s. It was NASA's

Lunar Roving Vehicle (LRV), shown in action on the moon in the images of Figure 1-1.

At a time when drivers on Earth navigated using paper road maps (assuming they could successfully unfold and refold them) and checked their oil, coolant, and tire pressure levels manually, the astronaut drivers of the LRV navigated on the moon by continuously sending data on direction and distance to a computer that calculated all-important insights needed for the mission. These included overall direction and distance back to the Lunar Module that would carry them home. This "connected car" could talk to Earth via audio or video transmissions. Operators at Mission Control were able to activate and direct the video camera on the LRV from their position on Earth, about a quarter million miles away.

Figure 1-1. Top: US NASA astronaut and mission commander Eugene A. Cernan performs a check on the LRV while on the surface of the moon during the Apollo 17 mission in 1972. The vehicle is stripped down in this photo prior to being loaded up for its mission. (Image

credit: NASA/astronaut Harrison H. Schmitt; in the public domain: http://bit.ly/lrv-apollo17.) Bottom: A fully equipped LRV on the moon during the Apollo 15 mission in 1971. This is a connected vehicle with a low-gain antenna for audio and a high-gain antenna to transmit video data back to Mission Control on Earth. (Image credit: NASA/ Dave Scott; cropped by User:Bubba73; in the public domain: http:// bit.ly/lvr-apollo15.)

Vehicle connectivity for Earth-bound cars has come a long way since the Apollo missions. Surprisingly, among the most requested services that automobile drivers want from their connectivity is to listen to their own music playlist or to more easily use their cell phone while they are driving—it's almost as though they want a cell phone on wheels. Other desired services for connected cars include being able to get software updates from the car manufacturer, such as an update to make warning signals operate correctly. Newer car models make use of environmental data for real-time adjustments in traction or steering. Data about the car's function can be used for predictive maintenance or to alert insurance companies about the driver and vehicle performance. (As of the date of writing this book, modern connected cars do not communicate with anyone on the moon, although they readily make use of 4G networks.)

Today's cars are also equipped with an event data recorder (EDR), also called a "black box," such as that well-known device on airplanes. Huge volumes of sensor data for a wide variety of parameters are collected and stored, mainly intended to be used in case of an accident or malfunction.

Connectivity is particularly important for high-performance automobiles. Formula I racecars are connected cars. Modern Formula I cars *measure hundreds of sensors* at up to 1 kHz (or even more with the latest technology) and transmit the data back to the pits via an RF link for analysis and forwarding back to headquarters.

Cars are not the only IoT-enabled vehicles. Trains, planes, and ships also make use of sensor data, GPS tracking, and more. For example, partnerships between British Railways, Cisco Systems, and telecommunication companies are building connected systems to reduce risk for British trains. Heavily equipped with sensors, the trains monitor the tracks, and the tracks monitor the trains while also communicating with operating centers. Data such as information about train speed, location, and function as well as track conditions are transmitted as continuous streams of data that make it possible for computer applications to provide low-latency insights as events happen. In this way, engineers are able to take action in a timely manner.

These examples underline one of the main benefits of real-time analysis of streaming data: the ability to respond quickly to events.

Streaming Data: Life As It Happens

The benefits of handling streaming data well are not limited to getting in-the-moment actionable insights, but that is one of the most widely recognized goals. There are many situations where in order for a response to be of value, it needs to happen quickly. Take for instance the situation of crowd-sourced navigation and traffic updates provided by the mobile application known as Waze. A view of this application is shown in Figure 1-2. Using real-time streaming input from millions of drivers, Waze reports current traffic and road information. These moment-to-moment insights allow drivers to make informed decisions about their route that can reduce gasoline usage, travel time, and aggravation.

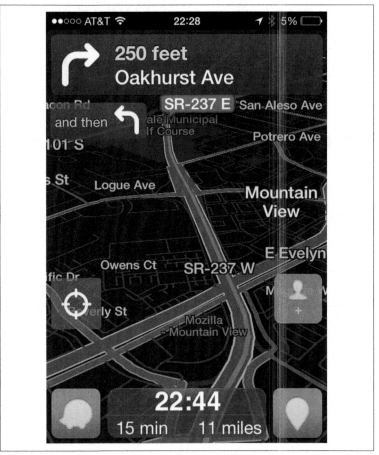

Figure 1-2. Display of a smartphone application known as Waze. In addition to providing point-to-point directions, it also adds value by supplying real-time traffic information shared by millions of drivers.

Knowing that there is a slow-down caused by an accident on a particular freeway during the morning commute is useful to a driver while the incident and its effect on traffic are happening. Knowing about this an hour after the event or at the end of the day, in contrast, has much less value, except perhaps as a way to review the history of traffic patterns. But these after-the-fact insights do little to help the morning commuter get to work faster. Waze is just one straightforward example of the *time-value of information*: the value of that particular knowledge decreases quickly with elapsed time. Being able to process streaming data via a 4G network and deliver reports to drivers in a timely manner is essential for this navigation tool to work as it is intended.

 Low-latency analysis of streaming data lets you respond to life as it happens.

Time-value of information is significant in many use cases where the value of particular insights diminishes very quickly after the event. The following section touches on a few more examples.

Where Streaming Matters

Let's start with retail marketing. Consider the opportunities for improving customer experience and raising a customer's tendency to buy something as they pass through a brick-and-mortar store. Perhaps the customer would be encouraged by a discount coupon, particularly if it were for an item or service that really appealed to them.

The idea of encouraging sales through coupons is certainly not new, but think of the evolution in style and effectiveness of how this marketing technique can be applied. In the somewhat distant past, discount coupons were mailed en masse to the public, with only very rough targeting in terms of large areas of population—very much a fire hose approach. Improvements were made when coupons were offered to a more selective mailing list based on other information about a customer's interests or activities. But even if the coupon was well-matched to the customer's interest, there was a large gap in time and focus between receiving it via mail or newspaper and being able to act on it by going to the store. That left plenty of time for the impact of the coupon to "wear off" as the customer became distracted by other issues, making even this targeted approach fairly hit-or-miss.

Now imagine instead that as a customer passes through a store, a display sign lights up as they pass to offer a nice selection of colors in a specific style of sweater or handbag that interests them. Perhaps a discount coupon code shows up on the customer's phone as they reach the electronics department. Or suppose the store is an outdoor outfitter that can distinguish customers who are interested in camping plus canoeing from those who like camping plus mountain biking, based on their past purchases or web-viewing habits. Beacons might react to the smartphones of customers as they enter and provide offers via text messages to their phones that fit these different tastes. How much more effective could a discount coupon be if it's offered not only to the right person but also *at just the right moment*?

These new approaches to customer-responsive, in-the-moment marketing are already being implemented by some large retail merchants, in some cases developed in-house and in others through vendors who provide innovative new services. The ability to recognize the presence of a particular customer may make use of a WiFi connection to a cell phone or sometimes via beacons placed strategically in a store. These techniques are not limited to retail stores. Hotels and other service organizations are also beginning to look at how these approaches can help them better recognize return customers or be alert to constantly changing levels needed for service at check-in or in the hotel lounge.

These approaches are not limited to retail marketing. Surprisingly, similar techniques can also be used to track the position of garbage trucks and how they service "smart" dumpsters that announce their relative fill levels. Trucks can be deployed on customized schedules that better match actual needs, thus optimizing operations with regard to drivers' time, gas consumption, and equipment usage.

The main goal in each of these sample situations is to gain actionable insights in a timely manner. The response to these insights may be made by humans or may be automated processes. Either way, timing is the key. The aim is to exploit streaming data and new technologies to be able to respond to life in the moment. But as it turns out, that's not the only advantage to be gained from using streaming data, as we discuss later in this chapter. It turns out that a streaming architecture forms the core for a wide-ranging set of processes, some of which you may not previously have thought of in terms of streaming.

One of the most important and widespread situations in which it is important to be able to carry out low-latency analytics on streaming data is for defending data security. With a well-designed project, it is possible to monitor a large variety of things that take place in a system. These actions might include the transactions involving a credit card or the sequence of events related to logins for a banking web-site. With anomaly detection techniques and very low-latency tech-nologies, cyber attacks by humans or robots may be discovered quickly so that action can be taken to thwart the intrusion or at least to mitigate loss.

Batch Versus Streaming

In the past, in order to handle data analysis at scale, data was collec-ted and analyzed in batch. What's the difference in a batch versus a streaming process? Consider for a moment this simple analogy: compare data to water that may be collected in a bucket and deliv-ered to the user versus water that flows to the user via a pipe.

It's possible to put a valve on the pipe such that the flow of water is periodically interrupted when the tap is closed. But with the pipe and valve, it is the choice of the user whether to hold back the water or to let it flow—it can handle both styles of delivery. In contrast, even if you carry buckets very quickly to the recipient, the water delivered by bucket (batch) will never occur as a continuous stream.

In computing, batch processing is a good way to deal with huge amounts of distributed data, and batch-based computational approaches such as MapReduce or Spark are still useful in many sit-uations. If you require an hourly summation of a series of events and an end-of-day or weekly final sum, batch processes may serve your needs well. But for many use cases, batch does not sufficiently reflect the way life happens. That observation underlies the increas-ing interest in flow-based computing, which is explained more thoroughly in Chapter 3.

As mentioned earlier, the benefits of adopting a streaming style of handling data go far beyond the opportunity to carry out real-time or near–real time analytics, as powerful as those immediate insights may be. Some of the broader advantages require durability: you need a message-passing system that persists the event stream data in such a way that you can apply checkpoints to let you restart reading from a specific point in the flow.

Beyond Real Time: More Benefits of Streaming Architecture

Industrial settings provide examples from the IoT where streaming data is of value in a variety of ways. Equipment such as pumps or turbines are now loaded with sensors providing a continuous stream of event data and measurements of many parameters in real or near-real time, and many new technologies and services are being developed to collect, transport, analyze, and store this flood of IoT data.

Modern manufacturing is undergoing its own revolution, with an emphasis on greater flexibility and the ability to more quickly respond to data-driven decisions and reconfigure to make appropriate changes to products or processes. Design, engineering, and production teams are to work much more closely together in future. Some of these innovative approaches are evident in the world-leading work of the University of Sheffield Advanced Manufacturing Centre with Boeing (AMRC) in northern England. A fully reconfigurable futuristic Factory 2050 is scheduled to open there in 2016. It is designed to enable production pods from different companies to "dock" on the factory's circular structure for additional customization. This facility is depicted in Figure 1-3.

Figure 1-3. Hub-and-spoke design of the fully reconfigurable Factory 2050, a revolutionary facility that is part of the AMRC. Its flexible interior layout will enable rapid changes in product design, a new style

in how manufacturing is done. (Image credit Bond Bryan Architects, used with permission.)

This move toward flexibility in manufacturing as part of the IoT is also reflected in the now widespread production of so-called "smart parts." The idea is that not only will sensor measurements on the factory floor during manufacture provide a fine-grained view of the manufacturing process, the parts being produced will also report back to the manufacturer after they are deployed to the field. This data informs the manufacturer of how well the part performs over its lifetime, which in turn can influence changes in design or manufacture. Additionally, these streams of smart-part reports are also a monetizable product themselves. Manufacturers may sell services that draw insights from this data or in some cases sell or license access to the data itself. What all this means is that streaming data is an essential part of the success of the IoT at many levels.

The value of streaming sensor data goes beyond real-time insights. Consider what happens when sensor data is examined along with long-term detailed maintenance histories for parts used in pumps or other industrial equipment. The event stream for the sensor data now acts as a "time machine" that lets you look back, with the help of machine learning models, to find anomalous patterns in measurement values prior to a failure. Combined with information from the parts' maintenance histories, potential failures can be noted long before the event, making predictive maintenance alerts possible before catastrophic failures can occur. This approach not only saves money; in some cases, it may save lives.

Emerging Best Practices for Streaming Architectures

An old way of thinking about streaming data is "use it and lose it." This approach assumed you would have an application for real-time analytics, such as a way to process information from the stream to create updates to a real-time dashboard, and then just discard the data. In cases where an upstream queuing system for messages was used, it was perhaps thought of only as a safety buffer to temporarily hold event data as it was ingested, serving as a short-term insurance against an interruption in the analytics application that was using the data stream. The idea was that the data in the event stream no longer had value beyond the real-time analytics or that there was no easy or affordable way to persist it, but that's changing.

While queuing is useful as a safety message, with the right messaging technology, it can serve as so much more. One thing that needs to change to gain the full benefit of streaming data is to discard the "use it and lose it" style of thinking.

 When it comes to streaming data, don't just use it and throw it away. Persistence of data streams has real benefits.

Being able to respond to life as it happens is a powerful advantage, and streaming systems can make that possible. For that to work efficiently, and in order to take advantage of the other benefits of a well-designed streaming system, it's necessary to look at more than just the computational frameworks and algorithms developed for real-time analytics. There has been a lot of excitement in recent years about low-latency in-memory frameworks, and understandably so. These stream processing analytics technologies are extremely important, and there are some excellent new tools now available, as we discuss in Chapter 2. However, for these to be used effectively you also need to have access to the appropriate data—you need to collect and transport data as streams. In the past, that was not a widespread practice. Now, however, that situation is changing and changing fast.

One of the reasons modern systems can now more easily handle streaming data is improvements in the way message-passing systems work. Highly effective messaging technologies collect streaming data from many sources—sometimes hundreds, thousands, or even millions—and *deliver it to multiple consumers of the data*, including but not limited to real-time applications. You need the effective message-passing capabilities as a fundamental aspect of your streaming infrastructure.

At the heart of modern streaming architecture design style is a messaging capability that uses many sources of streaming data and makes it available on demand by multiple consumers. An effective message-passing technology decouples the sources and consumers, which is a key to agility.

Healthcare Example with Data Streams

Healthcare provides a good example of the way multiple consumers might want to use the same data stream at *different times*. Figure 1-4 is a diagram showing several different ways that a stream of test results data might be used. In our healthcare example, there are multiple data sources coming from medical tests such as EKGs, blood panels, or MRI machines that feed in a stream of test results. Our stream of medical results is being handled by a modern-style messaging technology, depicted in the figure as a horizontal tube. The stream of medical test results data would not only include test outcomes, but also patient ID, test ID, and possibly equipment ID for the instrumentation used in the lab tests.

With streaming data, what may come to mind first is real-time analytics, so we have shown one consumer of the stream (labeled "A" in the figure) as a real-time application. In the older style of working with streaming data, the data might have been single-purpose: read by the real-time application and then discarded. But with the new design of streaming architecture, multiple consumers might make use of this data right away, in addition to the real-time analytics program. For example, group "B" consumers could include a database of patient electronic medical records and a database or search document for number of tests run with particular equipment (facilities management).

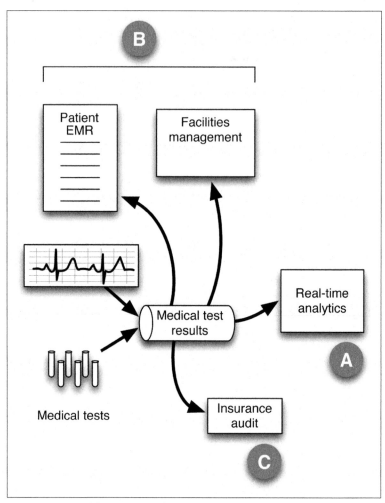

Figure 1-4. Healthcare example with streaming data used for more than just real-time analytics. The diagram shows a schematic design for a system that handles data from several sources such that it can be used in different ways and at different times by multiple consumers. The message-passing technology is represented here by the tube labeled with the content of the data stream (medical test results). EMR stands for electronic medical records. Note that the consumer in group C, the insurance audit, might not have been planned for when the system was designed or deployed.

One of the interesting aspects of this example is that we may want the data stream to serve as a durable, auditable record of the test results for several purposes, such as an insurance audit (labeled as use type "C" in the figure). This audit could happen at a later time and might even be unplanned. This is not a problem if the messaging software has the needed capabilities to support a durable, replayable record.

Streaming Data as a Central Aspect of Architectural Design

In this book, we explore the value of streaming data, explain why and how you can put it to good use, and suggest emerging best practices in the design of streaming architectures. The key ideas to keep in mind about building an effective system that exploits streaming data are the following:

1. Real-time analysis of streaming data can empower you to react to events and insights as they happen.

2. Streaming data does not need to be discarded: data persistence pays off in a variety of ways.

3. With the right technologies, it's possible to replicate streaming data to geo-distributed data centers.

4. An effective message-passing system is much more than a queue for a real-time application: it is the heart of an effective design for an overall big data architecture.

The latter three points (persistence of streaming data, geo-distributed replication, and the central importance of the correct messaging layer) are relatively new aspects of the preferred design for streaming architectures. Perhaps the most disruptive idea presented here is that streaming architecture should not be limited to specialized real-time applications. Instead, organizations benefit by adopting this streaming approach as an essential aspect of efficient, overall architecture.

CHAPTER 2

Stream-based Architecture

In the previous chapter, we looked at some of the reasons *why* so many people are getting interested in using streaming data. Now we explain the *how*—the ways to build a streaming system to best advantage.

Emerging technologies for message passing now make it possible to use streaming almost everywhere. This innovation is the biggest idea in this chapter.

Stream-based architecture provides great benefits when employed across any or all of the data activities for your enterprise.

The new designs we have in mind rely on a large-scale shift in the overall design approach you use to build systems. This transition is not just about acquiring a particular technology or the skill to use a certain fast algorithm—it is about change on a much broader and more fundamental level. It is also unusual among advances in system architecture in that it *can be introduced incrementally with accelerating benefits as you convert more and more services.*

A Limited View: Single Real-Time Application

The need for that level of overall change toward a streaming architecture may not be apparent to everyone right away. The initial lure to use streaming data may be a particular project or goal that requires real-time analytics. For example, suppose your organization is interested in building a dashboard for real-time updates. You might initially identify the streaming data source of interest and look for a powerful stream-processing software, such as Apache Spark Streaming. You like the in-memory aspect of this tool because it can provide near–real time processing, and that meets your particular goals. You'll export the results from this analytics application to the dashboard for almost–real time updates. You also like the idea that the raw streaming data can be analyzed right away, without needing to be saved to files or a database. Perhaps you're thinking this is all you need to build a successful project.

But suppose the analytics program has a temporary interruption or slow down. The incoming stream of data might be dropped. You want some insurance, so you also plan for a message queue to serve as a safety buffer as you ingest data en route to the Spark-based application. This type of design for a single-purpose data path for real-time stream processing is shown in Figure 2-1. For the purposes of this chapter, we will keep the examples generic to focus attention on the pattern of the design in each case.

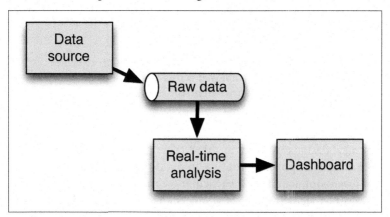

Figure 2-1. This diagram shows a simple design typical of how people have previously thought of using real-time analytics. In this example, data from a single source is used to update a real-time dashboard. The tube represents a messaging system employed for safety as data is ingested.

The plan shown in Figure 2-1 isn't a bad design, and with the right choice of tools to carry out the queuing and analytics and to build the dashboard, you'd be in fairly good shape *for this one goal.* But you'd be missing out on a much better way to design your system in order to take full advantage of the data and to improve your overall administration, operations, and development activities.

Instead, we recommend a radical change in how a system is designed. *The idea is to use data streams throughout your overall architecture*—data streaming becomes the default way to handle data rather than a specialty. The goal is to streamline (pun not intended) your whole operation such that data is more readily available to those who need it, when they need it, for real-time analytics and much more, without a great deal of inconvenient administrative burden.

Key Aspects of a Universal Stream-based Architecture

The idea that you can build applications to draw real-time insights from data before it is persisted is in itself a big change from traditional ways of handling data. Even machine learning models are being developed with streaming algorithms that can make decisions about data in real time and learn at the same time. Fast performance is important in these systems, so in-memory processing methods and technologies are attracting a lot of attention.

However, as mentioned in Chapter 1, the ability to analyze streaming data directly without having to first save it to files or a database does not mean that it's not useful to persist it—just that persistence can be done independently. That goes for other processing steps as well. With an overall stream-based approach that cuts across multiple systems like we are advocating, one important characteristic is that data can be used immediately upon ingestion, but it should not disappear if the downstream process is not ready for it when the data arrives. Messages should be *durable.*

In addition, these architectures need to handle very large volumes of data, so the tools used to implement them need to be *highly scalable* throughout the system. It's also important to design systems that can handle data from multiple data sources, making it available to a variety of data consumers.

"Data Integration means making available all the data that an organization has to all the services and systems that need it."[1]

—Jay Kreps

An important advantage of a system designed to use streaming data as part of overall data integration is the ability to change the system quickly in response to changing needs. *Decoupling* dependencies between data sources and data consumers is one key to gaining this flexibility, as explained more thoroughly in Chapter 3, which deals with streaming data and microservices.

A generalized view of these characteristics of a stream-based architecture is shown in Figure 2-2. Some details are omitted to keep the diagram simple. In this case, we've improved on as well as expanded the single-purpose design for real-time updates to a dashboard that was outlined in Figure 2-1. To make the comparison easy, the components that were present in Figure 2-1 are shown as shaded in Figure 2-2; the unshaded parts highlight additional projects as well as a modification of the original data flow for the real-time dashboard.

---

[1] *I Heart Logs* (*http://shop.oreilly.com/product/0636920034339.do*) (O'Reilly).

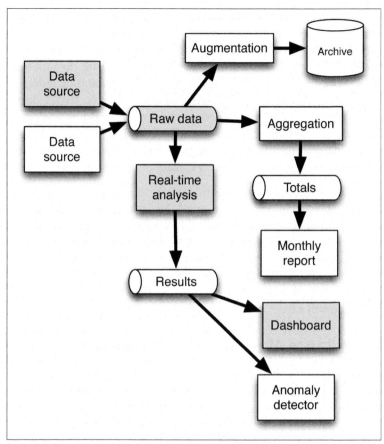

Figure 2-2. Concept of global design for streaming architecture: more than one component can make use of the same stream of messages for a variety of uses that go far beyond just real-time analytics. This design provides data integration, with stream messaging infrastructure throughout to deliver data as it is needed.

First of all, notice that the results of ▓▓▓▓▓ the real-time application now goes to a message stre▓▓▓▓▓ consumed by the dashboard rather than reaching the d▓ ▓board directly. In this way, the results can easily be used by an additional component, such as the anomaly detector shown in this hypothetical example. One nice feature of this style of design is that the anomaly detector can be added as an afterthought. The flexible system design lends itself to modifications without a great deal of administrative hassles or downtime.

Our overall design also takes into account the desire to use multiple data sources. Since the consumers of messages don't depend on the producers, they also don't depend on the *number* of producers. The messaging system also makes the raw data available to non–real time processes, such as those needed to produce a monthly report or to augment data prior to archiving in a database or search document. This happens because we assume the messaging system is durable. As in the healthcare example described in Chapter 1, our streaming architecture design supports a variety of applications and needs beyond just real-time processing.

As you think about how to build a streaming system and which technologies to choose, keep in mind the *capabilities required to support this design*. Tools and technologies change, and new ones are developed, particularly in response to the growing interest in these approaches. But the fundamental requirements of an effective streaming architecture are more constant, so it's important to first identify the basic needs of the system as you consider what technologies you will use.

Importance of the Messaging Technology

Message-passing infrastructure is at the heart of what makes this new approach work well. Let's examine some of the key capabilities of the messaging component if we are to take full advantage of the universal stream-based architecture presented in this book. To do that, think about what we've said about how the message-passing layer needs to work in our design, as represented in Figure 2-3.

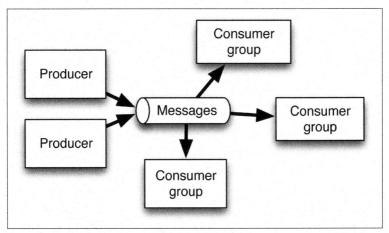

Figure 2-3. Messaging technologies such as the one represented by the tube in this diagram need to handle data from multiple data sources (producers) and make it available through subscription by groups of consumers in a decoupled manner.

You'll see terminology used in somewhat different ways when describing different systems, so please think in terms of the underlying meaning here. The data source is what sends a series of event data to the messaging system. It's sometimes called a *producer* or *publisher*. In our system, we expect the messaging technologies to handle messages from a huge number of producers.

The producer sends this event data without knowledge of the process that will make use of it. We call the thing that uses the messages the *consumer*, also sometimes called the *subscriber*. Each stream of messages is named (we call this the *topic*). The consumer (or a group of consumers) requests or subscribes to any topics it needs. We will say more about the details of these terms in Chapter 4 and Chapter 5. The beauty of this approach is that the messages can be sent whether or not the consumer ██████ receive them, and they stay available until the consumer is ready. That is an essential aspect of any messaging system we select. And for our design, the messaging software must be able to provide messages to multiple consumers.

Our architecture is also intended for projects using very large-scale data and requiring the ability to handle data at very high rates. Of course, if we want to use these systems in production, we also need to be confident that our messaging choice provides fault tolerance.

What characteristics, then, should we look for as being *essential* in our messaging technology if it is to support these needs?

Full independence of the producer and consumer
A messaging tool must not require that the producer know about the consumers that will process the messages.

Persistence
This is implied for full isolation of producer and consumer to work. Otherwise, messages will disappear if the producer and consumer are not coordinated to take the delivery as soon as the data appears.

Enormously high rates of messages/second
Extreme performance is required for modern use cases involving streaming data. If we want to use messaging as the core backbone of our systems, we have to handle huge message rates.

 It is unusual for message-passing systems to be able to maintain full isolation of producer/consumer with durability without sacrificing speed. However, to be appropriate for a universal stream-based architecture, these characteristics must exist together.

Naming of topics
This is not an unusual feature, but it is an important one, as it allows consumers to select the data they need.

A replayable sequence with strong ordering preserved in the stream of events
This is a highly desirable characteristic. Consumers can go back to whatever p̶ they wish to begin and read the sequence from that poin̶ ̶ ̶ ̶m restart a sequence. Producers can produce events an̶ ̶ ̶ow that they will be processed in order, thus allowing logical dependencies between events.

Fault tolerance
This characteristic is self-explanatory and required for critical systems.

Geo-distributed replication

This capability is not required in every use case, but in many cases it is an absolute requirement because the architecture needs to function across multiple data centers in different locations without sacrificing any of the above capabilities.

Where do we find messaging tools that can meet these strenuous requirements? There are two at present that are excellent choices to meet the needs of a universal stream-based architecture: Apache Kafka, which we describe in more detail in Chapter 4, and MapR Streams, which uses the Kafka API that we examine in Chapter 5.

 In a way, the choice of messaging tools organizes itself at present into two categories: the Kafka-related group (Kafka and MapR Streams) and the Others.

Messaging systems like Kafka work very differently than older message-passing systems such as Apache ActiveMQ or RabbitMQ. One big difference is that persistence was a high-cost, optional capability for older systems and typically decreased performance by as much as two orders of magnitude. In contrast, systems like Kafka or MapR Streams persist all messages automatically while still handling a gigabyte or more per second of message traffic per server. One big reason for the large discrepancy in performance is that Kafka and related systems do not support message-by-message acknowledgement. Instead, services read messages in order and simply occasionally update a cursor with the offset of the latest unread message. Furthermore, Kafka is focused specifically on message handling rather than providing data transformations or task scheduling. That limited scope helps Kafka achieve very high performance.

Choices for Real-Time Analytics

The development of a rich collection of technologies for processing streaming data, along with the evolution of effective, highly scalable messaging tools, is the driver for many more organizations to seek real-time insights from streaming data. In this book up until now, we have used the term "real time" to mean relatively low latency, but there are distinctions between technologies that approximate real time and those that actually analyze data as a real-time or very low-latency stream. For many applications, depending on SLAs, this distinction is not very important, but there are some situations in which "real-time" requirements are just that.

A detailed examination of technologies and methods for streaming analytics is beyond the scope of this short book, but we do provide an overview of desired capabilities and examine several choices, including how they differ. First we very briefly describe four technologies of interest: Apache Storm, Apache Spark Streaming, Apache Flink, and Apache Apex. Then, as we did for messaging, we take a look at some of the key capabilities for analytics that best support the stream-based architectures. We also compare some of the available technologies in the context of these capabilities.

A Confusion About Hadoop

The advent of fast, in-memory computational frameworks such as Apache Spark has led to some confusion about Apache Hadoop and the Hadoop ecosystem. You'll sometimes hear someone say, "Hadoop has been replaced by Spark," or wonder why Hadoop is still needed. Likely the reason they say this is that in-memory computational engines such as Spark are, in fact, taking the place of the batch-based computational framework of Hadoop known as MapReduce for many applications. Other parts of Hadoop, such as YARN and HDFS, are still widely used, however.

Confusion arises because people often make little distinction between Hadoop's MapReduce and the larger ecosystem of Hadoop-related technologies. Projects in the Hadoop ecosystem include Apache Spark, Apache Storm, Apache Flink, ElasticSearch, Apache Solr, Apache Drill, Apache Mahout, and more. These projects are leaders among very large-scale, cost-effective distributed systems.

What each project can do will change as they evolve. The qualities that best support streaming analytics, however, are relatively constant.

Given that each project's capabilities will continue to evolve, understand that the descriptions and comparisons of specific technologies are only general and represent a moment in time, but they should serve as an aide to help you think concretely about the features you'll want to look for.

Apache Storm

Apache Storm was a pioneer in real-time processing for large-scale distributed systems. The project website describes Storm as "doing for realtime processing what Hadoop did for batch processing." It's an accurate observation that the computational framework part of Hadoop, MapReduce, introduced a wide audience to batch processing at scale, and Storm added an early way to deal with real-time processing in the Hadoop ecosystem. The project Storm started outside of Apache under the leadership of Nathan Marz and has continued to evolve since it became a top-level Apache project.

Storm's approach is real-time processing of unbounded streams. It works with many languages. Recent additions intend to add windowing capabilities for Storm with an "at-least-once" guarantee, but historically, Storm has performed best with pure transformations or when windows could be defined at the application level rather than at the platform level. Storm's design has up to now involved what is known as "early assembly," in which rows are represented by Java objects that are actually constructed as they are read. This can limit performance relative to systems like Flink that use byte-code engineering to make it look like they are doing something else.

One of the challenges of distributed systems is that they are much more complex when it comes to making strong guarantees about correct operation in the presence of failures or intermittent operation. Some kinds of guarantees that can be made are at-least-once, at-most-once, and exactly-once. At-least-once processing means that every record is processed, but some may be processed more than once. At-most-once processing is roughly the opposite: no record will be processed more than once, but some records may be lost. Strictly speaking, it is impossible to unconditionally guarantee exactly-once processing, but if we can accept some restrictions, we can have guarantees that appear to be exactly-once and are good enough in practice. For instance, if the consumer uses messages to simply write (and never overwrite) a value in a database, then receiving a message more than once is no different than receiving it exactly once.

Apache Spark Streaming

Spark Streaming is one of the subprojects that comprise Apache Spark. Spark originated as a university-based project developed at UC Berkeley's AMPLab starting in 2009. The project entered the Apache Foundation in 2013 and became a top-level Apache project in 2014. In the last approximately three years, the overall Spark project has seen widespread interest and adoption.

Spark accelerated the evolution of computation in the Hadoop ecosystem by providing speed through an innovation that allowed data to be loaded into memory and then queried repeatedly. Spark Core uses an abstraction known as a Resilient Distributed Dataset (RDD). When jobs are too large for in-memory, Spark spills data to disk. Spark requires a distributed data storage system (such as Cassandra, HDFS, or MapR-FS) and a framework to manage it. Spark works with Java, Python, and Scala.

Spark Streaming uses microbatching to approximate real-time stream analytics. This means that a batch program is run at frequent intervals to process all recently arrived data together with state stored from previous data. Although this approach makes it inappropriate for low-latency ("real real-time") applications, it is a clever way to extend batch process to near–real time examples and works well for many situations. In addition, the same code can be used for batch processing applications as for streaming applications. Spark Streaming provides exactly-once guarantees more easily than a true real-time system. Where shorter latency (real-time) analytics are needed, people often employ a combination of tools with Spark Streaming/Spark Core plus Apache Storm for the real-time side of things.

Apache Flink

Apache Flink is a highly scalable, high-performance processing engine that can handle low latency as well as batch analytics. Flink is a relatively new project that originated as a joint effort of several German and Swedish universities under the name Stratosphere. The project changed its name to Flink (meaning "agile or swift" in German) when it entered incubation as an Apache project in 2015. Flink became a top-level Apache project later that year and now has an international team of collaborators. With increased public awareness, Flink's popularity grew rapidly in 2015, and some companies already use it in production.

Flink has the capability to handle the low-latency, real-time analytics applications for which Storm is appropriate as well as batch processing. In fact, Flink treats batch as a special example of streaming. Flink programs are developer friendly, they are written in Java or Scala, and they deliver exactly-once guarantees. Like Spark or Storm, Flink requires a distributed storage system. Flink has already demonstrated very high performance at scale, even while providing a real-time level of latency.

Apache Apex

Apache Apex is a scalable, high-performance processing engine that, like Apache Flink, is designed to provide both batch and low-latency stream processing. Apex started as an enterprise offering, DataTorrent RTS, but the core engine was made open source, and the project entered incubation at the Apache Software Foundation in summer of 2015. Apex describes itself as being "developed with YARN in mind." As such, it runs as a YARN application but avoids overlap in functionality with YARN. Apex supports programming in Java or Scala and was designed particularly to provide an easy way for Java programmers to build applications for data at scale as well as to reuse Java code. Like the other streaming analytics tools described here, Apex requires a storage platform. A particular advantage of Apex is the associated Malhar library of functions that cover a number of analytics needs.

Comparison of Capabilities for Streaming Analytics

Our description of tools for streaming analytics is neither exhaustive nor definitive. As we have said, all of these technologies are evolving, so descriptions of individual projects as well as comparisons of specific features and performance capabilities cannot remain accurate for long. That is in part why we encourage you to focus on the impact of capabilities for this style of architecture and to continue to assess different choices as they arise. That said, you may find it helpful to see a brief comparison of some key capabilities, which we provide here:

Fundamentals

Any technology used for analytics in this style of architecture needs to be highly scalable, capable of starting and stopping without losing information, and able to interface with messaging technologies with capabilities similar to Kafka and MapR Streams (described previously in this chapter).

Performance and low latency

These are relative terms, but for best practice, a modern architecture often needs to be designed to deal with batch and streaming applications even at very low latency, either to meet the requirements of existing applications or to be positioned to meet future needs. High performance is also usually a requirement.

 Technologies that can deliver processing that ranges from batch to low latency, as well as real-time processing without sacrificing performance, are attractive choices.

This observation does not mean that every situation requires very low-latency capabilities; indeed these are somewhat unusual, although they are becoming more common. A technology's features should meet the requirements of the current situation, but there is some advantage to building for future needs. At present, Flink and Apex probably have the strongest performance at very low latency of the given choices, with Storm providing a medium level of performance with real-time processing.

Exactly-once delivery

It is useful to provide exactly-once guarantees because many situations require them. For example, in financial examples such as credit card transactions, unintentionally processing an event twice is bad. Spark Streaming, Flink, and Apex all guarantee exactly-once processing. Storm works with at-least-once delivery. With the use of an extension called Trident, it is possible to reach exactly-once behavior with Storm, but this may cause some reduction in performance.

Windowing

This term refers to the time period over which aggregations are made in stream processing. Windowing can be defined in different ways, and these vary in their application to particular use cases. Time-based windowing groups together events that occur during a specific time interval, and is useful for asking questions such as, "how many transactions have taken place in the last minute?" Spark Streaming, Flink, and Apex all have configurable, time-based windowing capabilities. Windowing in Storm is a bit more primitive.

Time may not always be the best way to determine an aggregation window. For instance, it is common to divide visitor activity on a website into sessions separated by periods of inactivity of at least a specified length, typically 30 minutes. This makes time-based windowing less useful because not every session ends at the same time. Another way to define a window is to build programmatic triggers, which allow windows to vary in length, but still require synchronization of windows for different aggregations. Flink, Apex, and Spark do trigger-based windowing. Flink and Apex also do windowing based on the content of data.

Summary

A good design for streaming architecture can be a powerful advantage for you across all the data flow of your systems, not just for real-time analytics. The design calls for certain capabilities in terms of message passing, stream processing, and persistence. It's useful to understand the required or desired capabilities in order to assess the variety of tools that become available. Because this stream-based universal architectural design has at its heart a particular style of messaging, we will go into detail about the two technologies that currently best provide these capabilities—Apache Kafka (Chapter 4) and Kafka-based MapR Streams (Chapter 5)—but first we will examine in Chapter 3 why stream-based architecture strongly supports a style of computing known as microservices.

Streaming Architecture: Ideal Platform for Microservices

Over the last decade or so, there has been a strong movement toward a flexible style of building large systems that has lately been called *microservices*. This trend started earliest at innovative companies such as Google, and many aspects of microservices have since been reinvented at a variety of other companies. Now, among highly successful, fast-evolving companies that include Amazon, LinkedIn, and Netflix, the microservices approach has become more the rule than the exception, at least partly because companies who adopt this style of architecture move faster and compete better.

> "Instead of a big monolithic application, where every change is centrally coordinated, the new Netflix app is a series of microservices, each of which can be changed independently."[1]
>
> —Yevgeniy Sverdlik

The microservices idea is simple: larger systems should be built by decomposing their functions into relatively simple, single-purpose services that communicate via lightweight and simple techniques. Such services can be built and maintained by small, very efficient teams.

---

1 "Netflix Shuts Down Final Bits of Own Data Center Infrastructure" (*http://bit.ly/ netflix-microservices*)

Why Microservices Matter

Microservices are an important trend in building huge systems, primarily because the weak coupling between microservices allows agility even in large organizations. Here's how.

The evolution of the idea behind microservices started as a bit of a backlash against the complexity of service-oriented architecture (SOA) and the associated enterprise service bus (ESB) idea. The ideas behind SOA and ESBs have their roots in early mainframe development practices where there was a very strict class structure that determined who worked on different aspects of a system. With the advent of the Web, that class structure was reflected in the way that each tier in an *n*-tier architecture was designed and built by teams specialized in building a particular kind of tier. As these tiered systems grew larger, they were often broken into siloed systems, first by which business unit they served and then based on what rough function they served within a business unit.

The essence of this result was a tiered and siloed system as shown in Figure 3-1.

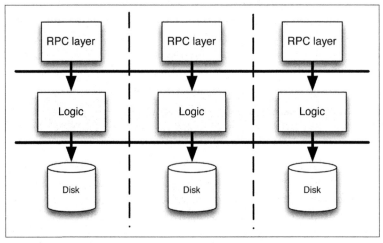

Figure 3-1. Traditional organization of large systems involved a horizontal segregation of components according to required skillsets, as shown here by horizontal lines. Further complications emerged as silos formed, as indicated by dotted vertical lines. Tier-oriented teams are not invested in individual systems because they are matrixed across multiple siloes. Isolation between systems is heavily compromised by this organizational structure and the architecture that echoes it.

The idea of SOA was to try to align each siloed system along functional boundaries and isolate their internal details. However, the complexity and rigidity of ESBs not only causes coupling between services, but also adds an entire level of difficulty to building these systems due to the requirement for coordinated changes. The resulting systems were difficult to build and maintain because changes in one part of the system often required changes in other parts. Performance was poor relative to the total investment because of the complexity of ESBs. These issues make SOAs much less effective in practice than it seemed in theory that they would be.

The emergence of highly scalable and more flexible systems such as Hadoop-based platforms has helped a lot by providing a cost-effective way to centralize large amounts of data for multi-tenant use. New data sources can also be used, and preparation of data for traditional systems happens in a more efficient and affordable way. This has tended to break down some of the siloes simply through collocation of data, but does not address the question of whether individual services could be made more independent and less coupled to other services and whether large systems could be built in an agile fashion, and that's where the microservices approach comes in.

 Microservices design makes use of focused teams that have a range of skillsets shared within the team.

The resulting systems do not have strong separations between tiers, but instead have cross-functional teams who are strongly aligned with the service they work on. The resulting systems are strongly isolated from each other, but the layers inside each system are not isolated. This idea is shown in the upper part of Figure 3-2.

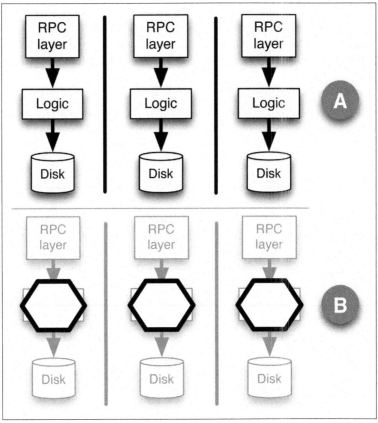

Figure 3-2. The evolution toward microservices breaks down the horizontal layers that segregate teams according to skills in older monolithic systems. Compare the upper part A of this figure to Figure 3-1, which depicts the older-style vision. Here the horizontal tiers have given way to cross-functional teams, each building a service. In the lower part B of the current figure, we represent each microservice being handled by a small team as an opaque hexagon to illustrate the idea that the internal details of a service do not matter.

The microservices approach involves building small services that interact only in limited ways via defined interfaces. In contrast to the older tiered approach that segregated skillsets, the microservices style breaks down the horizontal barriers and empowers a team to get the job done without burdensome negotiations and restrictions. An obvious benefit of this decomposition is that each service can be simpler, but the longer-term benefit stems from having small, cross-functional teams that behave more like startup development teams than enterprise software development teams.

 With microservices, you get the agility of a small team even in a large organization.

Somewhat surprisingly, the microservices teams are often charged not only with building the microservice, but also with operating it.

What Is Needed to Support Microservices

In order to carry out the goals of a particular cross-functional team, it's necessary to have effective communication between microservices, but this interaction needs to be kept lightweight and flexible. The goal is to give each team a job and a way to do it and get out of their way, as shown abstractly in Figure 3-3. The key idea is that services are opaque, and they communicate with only a few other services using lightweight, flexible protocols. This might entail using a remote procedure call (RPC) protocol such as REST or a messaging system such as Apache Kafka or MapR Streams. Data formats should be future-proofed by using JSON, Avro, Protobuf, Thrift, or a similarly flexible system to communicate.

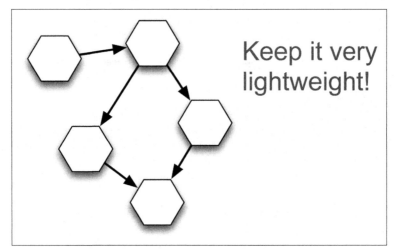

Figure 3-3. Microservices require a way to communicate between them, but it should be kept lightweight by using a REST API or by using Apache Kafka or MapR Streams.

The rise of microservices has also been paralleled by the rise in popularity of closely related ideas such as DevOps practices (where the team who built a service operates it), container systems like Docker (which make it easier to deploy self-sufficient versions of services), continuous integration (in which new versions of services are deployed quickly and often), and REST interfaces (which make it easy to build and document call-response services).

With a good streaming architecture, a microservices style of computing becomes a powerful approach that can be implemented much more easily.

Microservices in More Detail

Much of the discussion around microservices has stemmed from their early use in building complex websites, such as Netflix. As a result, much of the discussion has almost assumed that services interact using RPC mechanisms like REST involving a call and an immediate response. In fact, service interactions in a microservice architecture may need to use both synchronous call-and-response such as REST as well as asynchronous methods like message passing. Synchronous interactions tend to dominate the closer you get to a user (as with a website), while asynchronous service interactions become the rule as you move more toward analytical back-end systems where throughput becomes more important than response time and the desired analytical results are more and more the aggregation of many records. Applications designed to handle data from the IoT are often dominated by asynchronous service interactions.

Authors such as Martin Fowler and James Lewis (*http://bit.ly/smart-end-points-dumb-pipes*) emphasize that in microservice architectures, the data transport between services should be very lightweight. Instead of using elaborate enterprise service busses that can do lots of transformation and scheduling, microservice architectures should focus on so-called dumb pipes that do little more than transport data. In practice, the term lightweight should be interpreted to mean that the mechanisms used are *ubiquitous* and *self-service* for the teams using them.

Even though people tend to focus largely on the synchronous aspects of systems when describing microservice architectures, the asynchronous side deserves comparable attention. In fact, even in the case of a service that appears to involve a request that requires an immediate return result, what will often happen is that both kinds of processing will be involved. In such a combined action, something will be done immediately in order to be able to respond to the current request, but any work that can be deferred will be put into a message queue to be processed as soon as it is convenient to do so. Deferring work like this allows a much snappier user experience, but is also a way of decoupling the work schedules of different components of the overall system.

Flow Versus State

The transition from a large-scale monolithic application design using a large database to transactionally update and access state to a streaming microservice architecture can be difficult.

Much of the difficulty can be attributed to a switch from thinking of computer programs as state-oriented to thinking of them in terms of flows. Computation as a process that updates a global state is a very familiar idiom, but scaling such a system can be very difficult to do and often requires that a system be scaled up instead of out, which is a very expensive proposition.

Viewing computation as data flowing between independent processing elements is a less familiar idiom, but it has substantial benefits, perhaps most significantly that it is much easier to scale such a system out.

The key difference between the two systems is that state-based computation involves an idealized state that has a globally consistent value at any point in time. A simple example involves the question of the outside temperature at any given millisecond at many locations around the earth. We can't actually know what the temperature is at all of these locations, if only because light can only travel about 300 km in a millisecond. In fact, if we want to have carefully reviewed and cross-checked temperatures reliable enough for scientific publication, we will have to wait a month or more. This means that we can't build a computer program that assumes it knows all the current temperatures. We can, however, still write a useful program that knows the current local temperature and the delayed temperature from other locations.

Similarly, it isn't physically possible to actually have such a global state with modern computers without slowing computations to a crawl, but the illusion that such a state exists can often be maintained up to a certain size and at a certain time scale. Beyond that size or on a smaller time scale, maintaining the illusion becomes impossible (or at least fiendishly expensive).

Flow-based computation gets rid of the concept of global state and prevents parts from even pretending that the system knows exactly what other parts are doing. This allows more work to be done without coordination.

In this book, we focus on streaming architectures, that is, on asynchronous service interactions. We particularly address how recent developments in message-passing technologies such as Apache Kafka together with processing systems like Apache Spark, Apache Flink, and others make it possible to build more advanced streaming systems than ever before.

But before talking about specific messaging technologies that would enable microservices, let's look a bit more into what this all means to somebody designing or building such a system.

Designing a Streaming Architecture: Online Video Service Example

As an example of how to look at building a streaming architecture, especially from the point of view of microservices, let's examine part of a user-generated video website one of the authors built a few years ago and look at how we would build the site now with the advantage of a few more years of experience plus the appropriate modern tools for data streaming and flexible NoSQL databases to work with.

The basic idea of this system is that video files are uploaded by users and then processed to create everything needed to present these videos to other website visitors. This processing includes extracting video metadata such as size, length, original encoding, video resolution, date and time that the video was uploaded, and similar characteristics. The processing also includes the extraction of thumbnail images from different parts of the video and creation of different versions of the video suitable for streaming at different bit rates and resolutions to a variety of devices. A rough outline of the system as it was designed years ago is shown in Figure 3-4.

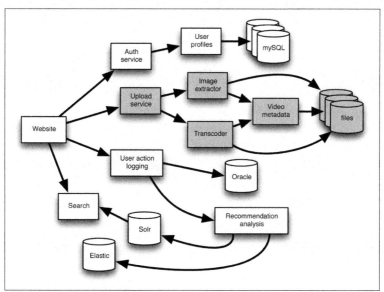

Figure 3-4. Original design of an online video service for a user-generated website. Here the arrows depict hand-coded custom data transfers that connect the different components or applications. Often

these connections were built using a variety of different technologies (even within one system), and these interchanges also made strong assumptions about timing and handshakes between the data source and recipient. There were strong dependencies between the components joined by arrows. Gray shading indicates part of the system shown in more detail in Figure 3-5. This pre-microservices system was very difficult to build and even harder to change.

This old-style system was difficult to build. One issue is that each arrow shown here connecting different components or processes was uniquely coded *ad hoc*, using different technologies from arrow to arrow. This traditional approach resulted in dependencies such that one piece affected many others: to make a change in the process at one end of the arrow or to add a new process required adjustments at the other end, which could cascade into more changes. The system was built and was successful, but at a considerable cost, and it lacked the agility needed to respond well to new ideas or changes in the marketplace.

A New Design: Infrastructure to Support Messaging

If we were to revisit this video system with a modern view toward taking advantage of microservices and the benefit of hindsight, we would use a different design. Let's see how implementation would be improved by using distributed files, a NoSQL database, and in particular an appropriate infrastructure to support communication between services.

Keep in mind that one of the main goals of microservices is to provide agility and ease of development. This requires isolation of service implementation details, and to support that, we would use a durable, high-performance messaging technology such as Apache Kafka or MapR Streams to provide the connections between components. This leads us to the system in Figure 3-5.

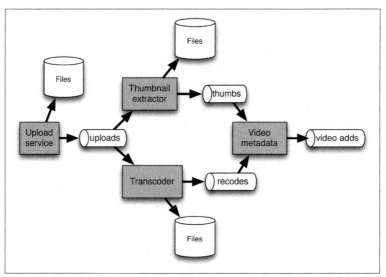

Figure 3-5. Use of messaging technology such as Apache Kafka or MapR Streams is shown here as horizontal tubes that are labeled with a description of the streaming data that they handle. These message streams form the connections between shaded microservices in this design. (For reference, see the shaded portion of the old design shown in Figure 3-4.)

There are a few important things that are not usually obvious to developers or architects getting started with this style of system. If we focus on just the thumbnail extraction service as in Figure 3-5, we see records are read from a stream called "uploads" and written to a stream called "thumbs." These labels indicate what data is available from that stream, much as a variable name should tell us what it contains. A new microservice can tap into the stream fairly easily to provide data or to consume it. This is an architectural design that provides agility.

Microservices can be implemented very quickly in an agile style by a small team precisely because of their very limited scope and restricted interfaces.

Also notice that videos are read from files and thumbnail images are written out as files on a distributed store so that other processes can access them. Subsequently, these microservices can be improved or possibly even completely reimplemented. New versions can be tested by running alongside the existing production version. Notably, microservices that work well enough need not be changed even as all the services around them change.

A key advantage of the right choice of message-passing technology is that it lets you avoid unwanted dependencies or complexities between services.

 For microservices to work as intended, they need to be connected by communication via durable, high-performance messages that decouple dependencies of each piece.

This move to use infrastructure to connect microservices together using asynchronous messaging is very different from connecting services using synchronous calls. In particular, with asynchronous messaging, there is no guarantee that the sender and receiver are even both running when the message is sent or when it is received, as mentioned in Chapter 2. In fact, there may well be times between the sending and receiving when neither sender nor receiver is running. This means that we have to have support for asynchronous messaging at an infrastructural level; we cannot depend on either the sender or receiver to handle the messages. Without infrastructure support for messaging, we will wind up with coupling between the implementation of the sender and receiver.

Very Short Latencies Require a Different Approach

The assumptions here break down a bit when dealing with systems that require very short (< 1ms) latencies. With very short latencies, both sender and receiver have to be running when the message is passed. That allows message passing to be handled differently from systems that have looser latency requirements, notably by using libraries like 0mq that connect sender directly to receiver. As latency requirements drop below about 100 microseconds, using direct connections becomes a requirement. This makes it harder to add consumers to existing flows, thus inhibiting the ability to inspect a running system. It also makes it much harder to avoid tight coupling between services, but not impossible.

Importance of a Universal Microarchitecture

Another aspect of building a streaming system is that every process-ing element really needs to have more than just the obvious inputs and outputs. For instance, taking the thumbnail extraction as an example again, the thumbnail extractor should also be sending information about normal operation such as number of videos pro-cessed, histograms of processing time, and so on to a metrics stream and should be sending records that describe processing exceptions to an exceptions stream. This is shown in Figure 3-6.

Metrics

For best practice, the components in a streaming system should use message streams as a way to collect metrics and exceptions throughout the system ubiquitously. Any service not worth monitoring isn't worth running.

This universal convention for collecting information like metrics and exceptions is known as a universal microarchitecture.

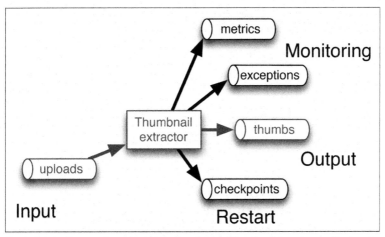

Figure 3-6. Processing elements should make use of a universal micro-architecture in which they emit metrics records and signal exceptions via well-known streams. Stateful processes may find it very useful to emit checkpoints to a stream to assist in reloading state on restarts and associating that state with an input message position so processing can be restarted correctly.

What's in a Name?

Another aspect of this architecture that might be surprising is that the naming of all data transfers seems a bit odd. Traditionally, when system diagrams like this were drawn in the past, an arrow was all that was necessary. No name was typically given. The implementation of each arrow depended on a convention agreed to between the source and the consumer. Typically, nearly every arrow used slightly different conventions, and this inconsistency led to a considerable amount of coupling between producers and consumers. Such a coupling violates the core premise of microservices and can ultimately result in a system that is almost as difficult to modify as a traditional ball of mud anti-architecture.

The right way to build a system like this is to support asynchronous message passing as an infrastructural capability so that all messages between services are passed using a consistent mechanism. Naming each connection facilitates connecting new consumers to a message stream. This idea is shown in Figure 3-7, where the depiction of infrastructure for message passing is simplified to just an arrow plus a label of the content of messages. In fact, the arrow is also an important component of the architecture, but when it functions well it essentially fades into the background of the design.

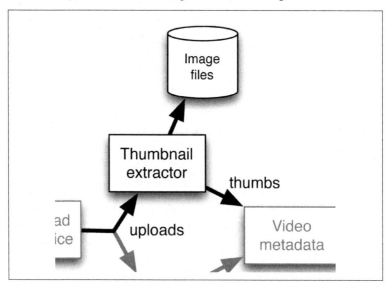

Figure 3-7. The thumbnail extraction service in isolation with its inputs and outputs. To make the diagram more concise and to allow us

to focus on noninfrastructural aspects, the message streams are shown as labeled arrows rather than tubes (as in Figure 3-5 and Figure 3-6). Note in this detail that the uploads *message stream has references to the original video files and the outgoing* thumbs *message stream includes references to the image files extracted by the thumbnail extraction process.*

Why Use Distributed Files and NoSQL Databases?

At a high level, if we are committing ourselves to using streams for connections between essentially all components and trying to keep state local as much as possible, then it seems like a contradiction to be storing thumbnail images as files in a distributed file system. In fact, while it is theoretically feasible to push all kinds of data through a message queue, files are still a very good solution for many purposes. If a good distributed file system is available, it can make systems that involve fairly large persistent data objects (more than a few megabytes) much simpler. This is true partly because many of the tools that we might use to process these objects, such as image extractors, or to serve them to users, such as web servers, assume that data is stored in files. It is much easier to just let these tools do what comes naturally. Also, Kafka, for instance, has a default maximum message size of only 1MB. MapR Streams caps message size at 2 GB. Neither limit is large enough to be sure that we won't need a file larger than that.

The file system can also be used to store checkpoints. A service can momentarily stop processing input while it writes data that is required to restart the process to files. In addition, the message offsets for all inputs can be stored so that processing can resume at the current point.

The use of distributed files and databases are shown in the new design for the video example that is explained in the next section.

New Design for the Video Service

Putting all these improvements together, we see how the modern design would play out for the video example. These changes include:

- Designing for a universal microservices architecture

- Maintaining independence of microservices by using lightweight communications between services via a uniform message-passing technology (such as Apache Kafka or MapR Streams) that is durable and high performance
- Use of distributed files, NoSQL databases, and snapshots

Now with this microservices and streaming approach in the new design, the purpose of each processing element in this architecture is apparent in Figure 3-8 and can be described in just a few sentences. More importantly, a prototype for each can be implemented in a few hours of work.

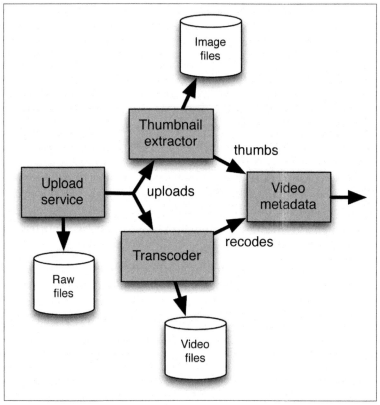

Figure 3-8. Modern design for the online video service example. Here we put all these ideas into practice in our example. Each processing element is represented by a rectangle. We indicate file or database persistence by a vertical cylinder. For simplicity, the connections between microservices that are supported by uniform messaging technology are shown by arrows labeled with the content of the stream, rather than

the tubular symbol used in Figure 3-5 and Figure 3-6. Note that this diagram is further simplified in that the metrics streams are not shown. Elements common to the old design are shaded.

For instance, the file upload service stores the raw video as a file in a distributed file store and sends out a record with information such as title along with the file name where the video data can be found. The thumbnail extractor reads these records and processes the video file to produce a number of image files and an augmented video record that now includes a list of the thumbnail files. The transcoder does a similar operation to produce versions of the video in different sizes and encoding qualities.

Records from the thumbnail extractor and transcoder are joined together to form a full description of the video (video metadata) and sent to processes that store this information into databases, thus providing convenient access for a variety of analysts. Note, too, that in addition to these description records being written to live databases, they can also be used to create snapshots of the database so that up-to-date copies of the metadata database can be created at will.

Summary: The Converged Platform View

For a microservices streaming architecture to work well, there are some constraints on how the platform that supports it has to work.

First, all of the services have to *use a consistent and ubiquitous transport mechanism for streaming data*. This is different from how synchronous microservices need to work because making a synchronous request to a service implies that the service itself can receive the query and provide the response. That means that you don't need much in the way of infrastructure to support synchronous microservices other than a solid network connection, but that approach limits flexibility and requires more administrative overhead.

Instead, we recommend asynchronous streaming services. With this streaming infrastructure approach, *the receiving service may not even be running when the message is sent to a stream*. This implies that it is important for the stream itself to be able to persist messages until they can be read and processed.

Another critical need is that new instances of the service will need to load any state that is being maintained by the service. This typically implies that old messages will need to be reread by this new instance as it gets ready to run, and that implies that those messages will need to stick around after the original instance of the service has already read them. Debugging or forensic examinations of services can also require that old messages be examined.

The current best practice for meeting these requirements is to use a replayable persistent messaging system such as Kafka or MapR Streams throughout a streaming system.

Many systems like the video processing chain described in this chapter manipulate large objects that can range from tens of megabytes in size to several gigabytes. While it is possible to write very large messages to messaging systems, it is usually considered bad practice. Large operations are better read or written using a file-like API with distinct open, read, write, and close operations. Message-passing APIs, on the other hand, typically require that an entire message be passed in a single call. This means that objects larger than a few megabytes should be passed by alternative methods, such as a distributed file system. The video processing chain does just this by writing the video files, thumbnail images, and converted videos to files and passing references to these files in messages.

The upshot of all of this is that successful implementation of a modern streaming architecture typically requires that Kafka-like message passing and a distributed file system be provided as a utility for all services. The adoption of a converged system that supports messaging, files, and tables makes asynchronous microservices much easier to build and maintain.

CHAPTER 4

Kafka as Streaming Transport

In Chapter 2, we established that at the heart of the revolution in design for streaming architectures is the capability for message passing that meets particular fundamental requirements for these large-scale systems. We recommended two technologies that are a good fit for the needed capabilities: Apache Kafka and MapR Streams. In this chapter, we examine in some detail Kafka, a pioneer in this style of messaging.

Motivations for Kafka

Apache Kafka started life as an engineering project at LinkedIn that was intended to bring order to the way that data moved between services. Most of the services at LinkedIn were originally designed to make heavy use of a relational database and to use remote method invocation (RMI) between Java processes where communication was necessary.

Unfortunately, both of these choices made it very difficult to deal with the rapid expansion of both the number of services and the amount of data being moved. Whenever one service needed to communicate with another, an adapter had to be developed and maintained. Moreover, each adapter tended to make the modification of both sender and receiver more difficult since every pair of communicating services effectively exposed a bit of the implementation of each to the other. The result was that it was incredibly difficult to update systems. Just as important, it was very difficult to move as much information between services as was needed.

Systems like SOAP, CORBA, or Java's RMI have long been based on the assumption that strict version control and strict type-safety were key to interprocess communication, but the experience of the LinkedIn team and many others over the last decade or so is very different. The crux of the problem that the LinkedIn team experienced is that as services start to communicate, if they use any form of strong typing contract on the interaction (such as a strictly versioned API, or a database schema), then each service acts as a bit of an anchor on further development or modification of the other service. Before long, the anchors can come to outweigh the services. These dependencies become a burden.

Realizing their predicament, the engineers at LinkedIn decided that they needed a consistent mechanism for communication between services that avoided the creeping problems they were facing. *It was clear that the communication had to be asynchronous and message-based.* In order to further decouple senders and receivers of messages, it was deemed important to have all messages persisted. This requirement for persistence combined with the required throughput, however, made conventional messaging systems infeasible in exactly the way that we saw in the previous chapter on microservices.

Kafka Innovations

Kafka adopted many of the basic ideas and much of the design of conventional message queues. Producers send messages to a message queue (or topic) that is identified by a topic name. Consumers read messages from topics and can arrange to be notified when any of a number of topics to which they subscribe have new messages.

There are, however, some key differences in how Kafka is built compared with older messaging systems. Key technical innovations have allowed Kafka to solve the problems of building a feasible message-passing layer for a large-scale service architecture.

Key technical innovations of Kafka:

Requiring all messages to be acknowledged in order.
 This eliminated the need to track acknowledgements on a per-message, per-listener basis and allowed a reader's operations to be very similar to reading a file.

Setting the expectation that messages would be persisted for days or even weeks.

This eliminated the requirement to track when readers have finished with particular messages by allowing the retention time to be set so long that readers are almost certain to be finished with messages before they are deleted.

Requiring consumers to manage the offset of the next message that they will process.

While the actual offsets for committed messages are stored by Kafka (using Apache Zookeeper), offsets for independent consumers are independent. Applications can even manage their offsets outside of Kafka entirely.

The technical impact of these innovations is that Kafka can write messages to a file system. The files are written sequentially as messages are produced, and they are read sequentially as messages are consumed. These design decisions mean that nonsequential reading or writing of files by a Kafka message broker is very, very rare, and that lets Kafka handle messages at very high speeds.

Kafka Basic Concepts

Before talking in detail about how to use Kafka, it is helpful to settle a bit on the players in a Kafka system and the roles they play. Overall, Kafka presents a particularly simple model to users, but the nomenclature may be a bit unfamiliar.

Think of these terms from the viewpoint of Kafka itself. *Producers* send messages to a Kafka *broker*, which is one server in a Kafka cluster. These messages can be read by consumers. This general arrangement is illustrated in Figure 4-1.

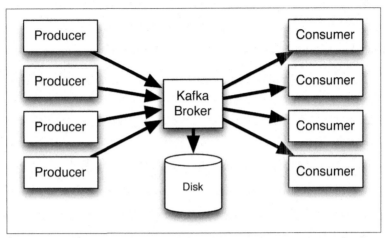

Figure 4-1. Producers send messages to the Kafka broker to be read by consumers. The broker persists the messages to a file system on disk for reliability and so that consumers can read the messages long after they are received by the broker.

A Kafka broker is responsible for taking care of messages in transit. *Messages* contain bytes in an application-defined serialized format and are associated by the producer with a *topic*, which is a high-level abstraction for grouping messages.

The use of a topic helps the consumers of messages find messages of interest without having to read lots of uninteresting messages.

The broker stores and forwards messages for many topics, and messages can be sent to a single topic by multiple producers. The producer will buffer a number of messages before actually sending them to the Kafka broker. The degree to which messages are buffered before sending can be controlled by the producer by limiting either the number of messages to buffer or the time that messages are allowed to linger before being sent.

Ordering

A *consumer* ultimately reads these messages. In the simplest case, all messages sent to a topic are read by a single consumer in the order that the broker received them. If it is necessary to have higher throughput in consuming messages, it is possible to divide a topic into multiple *partitions*. When this is done, the consumer can use multiple threads that may even be spread across multiple processes to read the messages from a topic, but the ordering of messages in a topic will only be preserved within a single partition, and the number of threads cannot be larger than the number of partitions. The producer can control the assignment of messages to partitions directly by specifying a partition or indirectly by specifying a key whose hash determines the partition.

Importantly, *messages in a topic partition are ordered*, and there is no provision for consumers to acknowledge individual messages out of order. A consumer has a read point that determines which message will be read next. Reading messages advances that read point automatically, but the read point can also be explicitly set to the start of any specific message, to the earliest message the broker has or to the end of the latest message that the broker has. Even so, the messages after the read point are read in order until the read point is explicitly repositioned. This file-like API is very different from the traditional sort of message queuing API in which messages can be read and acknowledged in any order.

Persistence

Another major difference between Kafka and traditional messaging systems is that persistence of messages is unconditional. Moreover, messages are retained or discarded in the order they were received according to the retention policy of the topic, without any regard paid to whether particular consumers have consumed the message yet.

The one exception is that when old messages in a topic are about to be deleted, they can be *compacted* instead. With compaction, a message is retained if no later message has been received with the same key, but deleted otherwise. The purpose of compaction is to allow a topic to store updates to a key-value database without unbounded growth. When a single key has been updated many times, only the latest update matters, since any previous update would have been overwritten by the last update (at least). With compaction, a topic cannot grow much larger than the table being updated, and since all access to the topic is in time order, very simple methods can be used to store the topic.

The Kafka APIs

Kafka's APIs have undergone a significant evolution over time. Originally, the APIs were very bare-bones, with significant complexity forced back onto the programs using Kafka. Subsequently, separate low- and high-level APIs were developed, but there was never a clear separation between the two, and it was common to need to use both high- and low-level APIs to accomplish fairly standard tasks.

With the recent 0.9 release of Kafka, the low- and high-level APIs have been merged into a single coherent API that simplifies how clients need to be written. This makes using Kafka considerably more intuitive. All new applications should use the 0.9 APIs (or later versions as they are released) if at all possible.

Sample Kafka Programs

This section covers the basic outlines of the Kafka 0.9 API, with some hints on tuning for performance, but we do not try to describe the details of how to code applications for Kafka here. We have written some sample programs and made them available to you via GitHub. You can find a blog with detailed examples on how to code for Kafka's 0.9 API with a link to the associated GitHub repository containing the sample applications at *http://bit.ly/ apache-kafka-code-samples*. You can also find detailed documentation on the API on the Apache Kafka website (*http:// kafka.apache.org/*).

KafkaProducer API

With Kafka, all messages to consumers are sent via the broker by using a KafkaProducer. As they are sent, messages are assigned to topics by the sending process. Within topics, messages are assigned to partitions either explicitly or implicitly via the hashcode of the key associated with the message.

Each instance of a KafkaProducer represents a separate connection to the Kafka broker, but there is typically little or no speed advantage to having multiple instances. Each KafkaProducer is thread-safe, so no special consideration is needed when using a single instance in multiple threads.

All messages in Kafka are sent asynchronously; that is, the messages are not actually sent over the network to the broker until some time after they are given to the KafkaProducer to send. Instead, they are buffered until the buffer fills (buffer.size in the Kafka configuration), or until a specified time period has passed (linger.ms in the Kafka configuration). By default, the buffer size and timeout are set quite low, which can impair throughput, but tends to give fairly good latency.

When data is sent from the producer to Kafka, there are differing degrees of durability guarantees that are possible via different configurations. These are controlled primarily by the acks (in the producer configuration) and min.insync.replicas (in the topic level configuration). At the lowest level, a message only needs to be sent before being acknowledged. Slightly better than this, you can require that a message be acknowledged by at least one broker. At the highest level, all brokers holding up-to-date replicas of a topic must acknowledge the receipt of a message.

Generally, we would strongly recommend starting with min.insync.replicas=2 and acks=all. The result is that all acknowledged messages will be on all of the up-to-date copies of a topic, and there will always be at least two such brokers for all acknowledged messages. This policy is similar to the policy used in the MapR file system and guarantees that if at least one up-to-date replica survives, no data loss will occur. Further, no single node or disk failure will cause loss of acknowledged messages.

There are a number of apparently performance-related properties that can be manipulated for a KafkaProducer. Mostly, the defaults for these are adjusted for good latency, but very moderate changes to just a few parameters can substantially improve performance. In particular, it helps to buffer more records (controlled by batch.size) and to wait a short bit before sending those buffered records off to the broker (controlled by linger.ms). For throughput-sensitive applications, increasing these parameters to 1 MB and 10 milliseconds, respectively, has a substantial impact on performance. For instance, in a small benchmark, 4 seconds were used in creating 1 million records without sending them, and it took

24 seconds to create and send them using the default parameters. Changing batch.size and linger.ms as recommended here decreased the runtime to about 8 seconds for about a 5x improvement in throughput. Increasing the parameters well beyond these settings had essentially no effect. Your results with real applications will differ, but it is clear that more buffering and just a bit more lingering have a substantial impact.

Once you have a KafkaProducer object, you can send messages to the broker using the send and flush methods. The send method simply copies the message to an internal buffer, which is automatically sent to the broker according to the policies applied to the Kaf kaProducer or when flush is called explicitly. Note that because the send method is completely asynchronous, there is no way for it to return the result of trying to send a message to the broker. The send method does, however, return a future that you can wait for, and there is a version that allows a callback to be passed with the message being sent. Both the returned future and the callback can be used to determine whether a message was sent successfully.

As we mentioned earlier, each message sent to the broker winds up in one of the partitions of the topic that it is sent to. The producer that sends the message gets to decide how the partition is chosen based on which version of the send method it uses. The partition can be specified directly and explicitly by providing the partition number, or the hashcode of a key value or a round-robin assignment to partitions.

When you are sending lots of data to the broker, it will likely not help to call flush, since the data is going to be flushed very shortly in any case due to the amount of messages being sent. On the other hand, when you are sending very few messages, it may improve latency a bit to explicitly call flush. flush also helps if you need to know that messages have arrived at the broker before sending other messages. The GitHub project (*https://github.com/mapr-demos/ kafka-sample-programs*) contains a simple message producer in the com.mapr.examples.Producer class.

KafkaConsumer API

In many ways, the consumer side of Kafka is trickier to code well than the producer side. The major areas that people have trouble with are the concept of consumer groups as they relate to partitioning of topics, the question of which messages have been processed by a failed process, and how consumer configurations can have surprising effects on the level of throughput that a consumer can achieve.

The point of consumer groups is to allow a controllable mixture between universal broadcast of all messages (which is helpful for adding new kinds of message consumers) and designating a single handler for each message (which is helpful for implementing parallelism in processing messages). Kafka uses the concept of a consumer group to mediate between these two extremes. All messages go to all consumer groups who subscribe to a topic, but within a consumer group only one consumer handles each message.

In addition, rather than allowing complete flexibility about which messages are sent to which consumers, Kafka requires that a topic be divided into partitions at the point of production. Thus, the producer of a message decides which topic and which partition a message is sent to, but the consumer group designates exactly which consumers handle which partitions of a topic.

The relationship of producers, topics, partitions, consumer groups, and consumers is illustrated in Figure 4-2.

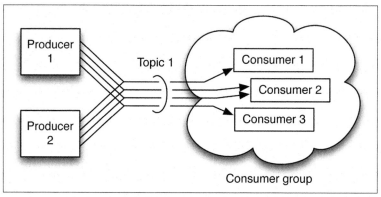

Figure 4-2. The producers determine which partition of a topic each message is sent to, and each partition is assigned to one consumer in each consumer group that is subscribed to a topic. Here, the topic is represented by parallel lines, each of which represents a partition of the topic. Routing partitions to different consumers allows parallelism to be used in processing messages, but ordering suffers since messages in different partitions may be subjected to different delay even while the messages within a partition remain ordered.

While Kafka provides ordering guarantees for messages within a single topic partition, applications should be careful about depending too much on transaction ordering. In Figure 4-2, for instance, messages *m1* and *m2* might be sent from producer1 on the same partition as used by producer2 to send messages *m3* and *m4*. If this happens, *m1* will always arrive to whichever consumer receives it before *m2* arrives, but it is very hard to make any statement about whether *m1* arrives before or after *m3*. It is best to code very defensively in such situations. If both producers are running on the same node, this should be easy, but if they are not, then it may be worthwhile investing in very high-precision clock synchronization.

One of the best defenses against confused ordering is a high-precision clock.

Another major confusion that new users have when writing a consumer has to do with the idea that messages may have been consumed, but not yet acknowledged by the consumer to have been consumed. The confusion comes from the fact that individual consumers keep track of the offset of the next message to be read, but they don't write that offset back to Kafka very often because it can be expensive for the broker to keep track of these updates. Kafka uses the terms "current offset" and "committed offset" to describe these two concepts. If a consumer continues to process messages in an orderly fashion and ultimately exits in a well-behaved manner by committing the current offset, then there won't be any problems. The fact that the current offset is ahead of the committed offset much of the time just won't matter.

On the other hand, if a consumer crashes without committing its offset back to the broker, then when another consumer starts processing the same partition, it will start from the previously committed offset, thus running the risk of processing messages twice (if the offset is committed after processing a batch of messages) or not at all (if the offset is committed before processing a batch of messages). Since it is generally impossible to make the processing of messages and the committing of the offset into a single atomic operation, there is pretty much always going to be a risk of not processing all messages exactly once.

The final confusion that strikes newcomers is the way a consumer decides what to read.

Default parameters that define how the consumer decides what to read and when to read it are tuned in Kafka 0.9 for low latency on topics that do not have a large amount of messages per second. This tuning can lead to problems like the one shown in Figure 4-3, where throughput is high for a short time, but then crashes for several seconds.

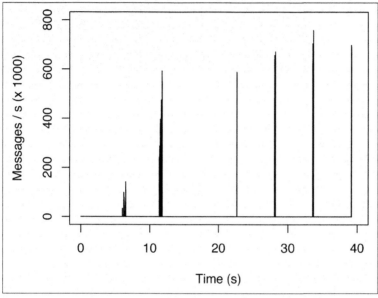

Figure 4-3. With the default setting for `receive.buffer.bytes,` *throughput rates are unstable and the consumer is unable to keep up.*

The key to dealing with this kind of instability is to set `receive.buffer.bytes` to a large enough value so that processing can proceed at a sustained high rate. It is also common to need to increase the values of `fetch.min.bytes` and `max.parti tion.fetch.bytes`. Figure 4-4 shows how much better things can be when these consumer configuration values are set appropriately.

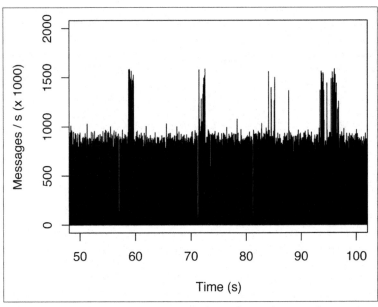

Figure 4-4. Setting the consumer's configuration values results in con-siderably higher throughput numbers. The throughput is still somewhat unstable on time scale of 100 milliseconds, visible by the way the throughput jumps up and down so much that the graph appears to be a solid mass of black, but average throughput is much higher than before.

Legacy APIs

One potentially confusing aspect of the most recent release is that Kafka retains an older API for consumers that is a melding of a very old API and a newer API that did not completely replace the func-tionality of the old API. This results in a confused programming model. More importantly, the old API exposed access to the imple-mentation details of Kafka in ways that seriously hampered efforts to improve performance and made it particularly difficult to improve reliability and security.

The older API has been retained in the 0.9 release, but should not be used for new applications. Instead, the newer style of interaction, often called the 0.9 API should be used. The sample programs we wrote (*https://github.com/mapr-demos/kafka-sample-programs*) are good examples of the basics of how to use the 0.9 API.

Kafka Utility Programs

Kafka comes with a variety of utility programs that help administer a Kafka cluster as well as some basic diagnostics. These utility programs can be used to start broker processes, create topics, move partitions or topics around in a cluster, and inject or display messages in a topic.

Two areas of particular importance have to do with (a) balancing of partitions and loading across a cluster and (b) the mirroring of topics to other clusters.

Load Balancing

Kafka has a particularly simple model in which each partition in a topic resides in its entirety on a broker, possibly with several other brokers acting as replicas of that partition. Partitions cannot be split across machines. This can become a serious problem because Kafka does not automatically move partitions to balance the amount of load or space on brokers. Likewise, if you add new nodes to a cluster, you have to migrate data to these new nodes manually. This can be a tricky and labor-intensive task since it is difficult to estimate which partitions are likely to grow or cause high loads.

Mirroring

Mirroring of data between Kafka clusters can be done using a utility called MirrorMaker. When it is run, MirrorMaker starts a number of threads that each subscribe to the topics found in a Kafka cluster. Multiple MirrorMaker processes can be run on different machines to get the benefits of higher parallelism and failure tolerance. Each MirrorMaker thread consists of a consumer that reads from the Kafka source cluster and a producer that writes to the destination cluster. There can be multiple source clusters. MirrorMaker makes use of consumer groups to allow traffic to be balanced across threads and servers.

There are some things that you should watch out for with Kafka mirroring, however.

With Kafka, there is no inherent connection between the source and the destination clusters other than the fact that messages that are written into a mirrored topic in the source cluster will be read from that topic by MirrorMaker and then sent to the same topic in the destination cluster. Offsets and consumer read offsets will not be preserved, and the mirror cannot be used as a fallback for consumers in a disaster recovery situation. Offsets will not be preserved, and the mirror cannot be used as a fallback for consumers in a disaster recovery situation.

For the same reasons, mirroring of any topic in Kafka has to be set up as a tree rather than as a general graph. The major issue is that if there are any cycles in the replication pattern, the amount of traffic will grow exponentially because duplicates are not detected during mirroring.

Kafka Gotchas

Kafka has made a huge difference in how easy it is to realize the promise of streaming architectures, but it is still a work in progress. Kafka is hampered in some respects by the fact that it is building from a very low foundation with respect to features such as data replication, fault tolerance, and geo-replication. This situation makes progress on some capabilities challenging.

That said, Kafka has made huge progress in a short time and clearly fills an important role, at least partially. Kafka is particularly good on first impression, and understandably so. You can download Kafka, check out a sample program, and have a sample application running in well under 10 minutes (I just checked).

Kafka also scales very well, simplifies the design of large systems, and is relatively easy to use, especially with the 0.9 API. It's no wonder that Kafka has a large and growing community of users. What's not to like?

Kafka in Production Settings

There are a fair number of significant issues that can crop up with Kafka as it goes into production at scale. Some of these issues are inherent in the current design of Kafka and are unlikely to change in the near future. Others are more likely to get better over time.

Limited Number of Topics and Partitions

The number of topics that can be handled by a Kafka cluster has a soft limit that starts to degrade operations at around a thousand topics. These problems are likely substantially tied to the fundamental implementation decisions that underpin how Kafka works. In particular, as the number of topics increases, the amount of random I/O that is imposed on the broker increases dramatically because each topic partition write is essentially a separate file append operation. This becomes more and more problematic as the number of partitions increases and is very difficult to fix without Kafka taking over the scheduling of I/O. Just above the current limits on number of partitions, there are likely other limits waiting, some fairly serious. In particular, the number of file descriptors that a single process can open is typically limited.

In order to be better prepared for production settings, Kafka needs to solve most of the problems inherent in file system design. That could well take several years of persistent effort to fix.

Keep in mind that the practical impact of having a limited number of topics varies by application and design. Most applications using Kafka so far have little trouble with the limit. The limitation may be more of an issue when Kafka is used as a multi-tenant resource since different users are likely to each want to use a fair number of topics themselves.

A limit on the number of topics also constrains the solution space that you can use and prevents Kafka from being a primary or archival store for many applications. For instance, if you are an electrical utility doing smart metering, it would be plausible to design a system in which each meter has a separate topic. The question of such a design is moot with Kafka, however, because having millions to hundreds of millions of topics is just not plausible.

Manual Balancing of Partitions and Load

Partition replicas in Kafka must each fit on a single machine and cannot be split across multiple machines. As partitions grow, it is expected that some machine in your Kafka cluster will have the bad luck of having multiple large partitions assigned to it. Kafka doesn't have any automated mechanism for moving these partitions around, however, so you have to manage this yourself. Monitoring disk space, diagnosing which partitions are causing the problem, and then determining a good place to move the partition are all manual management tasks that can't be ignored for a production Kafka cluster.

This sort of management can work when clusters are relatively small and data is small with respect to available space, but it can also become completely unmanageable if your traffic is subject to rapid growth or you don't have top-flight system administrators. Even worse, any instability in this respect or perceived competition for resources can cause DevOps teams to switch to using their own Kafka clusters, thus defeating the entire point of streaming data as an infrastructural resource. The requirement that all replicas of a partition must fit on all of the brokers holding it also makes Kafka unattractive for long-term archiving of data.

Fixing this will require a number of fundamental revamps to Kafka's architecture, but it is plausible that the basic implementation of Kafka could be changed so that the files that make up a partition are not constrained to being on a single machine. Doing this well would mean that the brokers in a cluster would have to maintain knowledge not only about where the master broker for a partition is, but would instead would have to remember where every small segment of every topic partition is located and which broker is serving as master for the current segment.

Doing this housekeeping is plausible, but would require a substantial effort to fix, and there are number of subtle points in handling this well. The issue of load and space balancing is handled differently with MapR Streams technology, as we'll describe in Chapter 5.

No Inherent Serialization Mechanism

Kafka doesn't have a favored solution to the problem of serializing data structures. This means that different developers tend to pick different serialization methods. It is crucial to successful use of Kafka that there be consistency in how messages are serialized between services that need to communicate.

The general argument against having a favored serialization convention is typically based on worries about performance of any general mechanism and about not having the benefit of future developments. In the context of a single organization, the arguments often boil down to issues of traditional usage. If there is a strong culture and established expertise that already supports one serialization framework, it is hard to imagine that a different serialization framework would be better enough to justify having a second framework.

On the other hand, having all serialization be external to Kafka forces data to be copied at least one more time than necessary. This can substantially impair performance of the messaging system.

Regardless of whether Kafka should have a strong convention in favor of one serialization system or another, it is imperative that each organization have a strong preference to avoid a messaging Babel. The gotcha isn't so much a system issue as a social one.

Establishing a strong convention early pays huge dividends later.

Mirroring Deficiencies

The mirroring system used in Kafka is very simple—and for many enterprise applications, a bit too simple. By simply forwarding messages to the mirror cluster, the offsets in the source cluster become useless in the destination. This means that producers and consumers cannot fail over from one cluster to a mirror. This ability to fail over is often considered required table stakes in enterprise systems and not having it may completely preclude getting the benefits of Kafka.

Kafka's mirroring design could cause similar headaches in the design of a chain of replication. Because the source cluster and the mirror don't really know anything about each other, any cycle in the replication of messages from cluster to cluster will cause messages to be mirrored over and over. Disaster will follow in short order.

Mirroring without cycles and without splits means that the replication pattern is a tree, and that is a very brittle design. Practically by definition, losing any link in a tree causes a partition. Worse, because of the ad hoc nature of mirroring in Kafka, it is essentially impossible to route around a lost step in a replication chain. This means that while data may be mostly preserved in these situations, it may not be clear which data is preserved.

The lack of cycles in mirroring patterns in Kafka also means that mirroring cannot be used to create multi-master systems in which you can pick any mirror to update. Multi-master replication is often considered a critical requirement in enterprise settings. Mirroring is handled very differently in MapR Streams, and a comparison may be useful.

Summary

Kafka has broken new ground as an early and innovative solution for streaming architecture. Kafka satisfies many of the requirements for high-throughput, single data–center messaging in support of microservice architectures. The API introduced in the 0.9 release is easy to use. Kafka does, however, require significant amounts of care and watering to manually manage storage space and distribution.

Given the strength of this design, there is naturally widespread interest in Kafka and Kafka-esque approaches. For multi-data center deployment, you may find that Kafka has significant issues. In those situations, keep in mind that programs written with the Kafka 0.9 API also run on MapR Streams. That flexibility in the Kafka API may provide a solution for the issues associated with running Kafka in a geo-distributed setting.

CHAPTER 5

MapR Streams

A second option for a messaging system that supports the requirements of a stream-based architecture is MapR Streams. Developed
as a ground-up reimplementation of the Apache Kafka API, MapR
Streams provides the same basic functions of Kafka but also some
additional capabilities, as we'll discuss in this chapter. MapR Streams
is integrated into the MapR converged data platform, and it is compatible with the Kafka 0.9 API. Most programs written to run on
that API will also run efficiently, without change, on MapR Streams.
If you know how to use Kafka, you'll have a head start on under-
standing how to use Streams. If you are not familiar with Apache
Kafka, you may want to review the previous chapter.

Innovations in MapR Streams

Although similar to Kafka, MapR Streams enables you to do some
very different things. At a high level, the differences include running
a much larger number of topics and applying policies such as time-
to-live or controlled access to many topics as a group. (Such a group
of topics in MapR is called a *stream*, as described later.) The ability
to set up a very large number of topics in MapR Streams lets you
build topics that reflect business goals rather than infrastructural
limitations. This capability allows a good fit between architecture
and the business problem being addressed.

Integration of the MapR messaging system into the MapR converged
data platform means less administration than is required when the
messaging technology is run on a separate cluster. Integration also

makes it easier to write end-to-end applications, and it lets you operate under the same security system for streams, files, and databases.

Another significant innovation of MapR Streams is geo-distributed replication. This capability makes it possible for you to share streaming data between multiple data centers, even in distant locations. This type of replication means you can update a topic at any of several locations and see the effects at all of your data centers. Geo-distribution via the messaging system is a powerful option that expands stream-based design to some interesting use cases, an example of which is described in Chapter 7.

Here is a more detailed explanation of the differences you'll find with MapR Streams:

1. MapR Streams includes a new file system object type known as a *stream* that has no parallel in Kafka. Streams are first-class objects in the MapR file system, alongside files, directories, links, and NoSQL tables.

2. A Kafka cluster consists of a number of server processes called *brokers* that collectively manage message topics, while a MapR cluster has no equivalent of a broker.

3. Topics and partitions are stored in the stream objects on a MapR cluster. There is no equivalent of a stream in a Kafka cluster since topics and partitions are the only visible objects.

4. Each MapR stream can contain hundreds of thousands or more topics and partitions, and each MapR cluster can have millions of streams. In comparison, it is not considered good practice to have more than about a thousand partitions on any single Kafka broker.

5. MapR streams can be replicated to different clusters across intermittent network connections. The replication pattern can contain cycles without causing problems, and streams can be updated in multiple locations at once. Message offsets are preserved in all such replicated copies.

6. The distribution of topic partitions and portions of partitions across a MapR cluster is completely automated, with no administrative actions required. This is different from Kafka, where it is assumed that administrators will manually reposition partition replicas in many situations.

7. The streams in a MapR cluster inherit all of the security, permissioning, and disaster-recovery capabilities of the basic MapR platform.

8. Most configuration parameters for producers and consumers that are used by Kafka are not supported by MapR Streams.

These differences can have a large impact when you are architecting a large system, but when writing a program for MapR Streams, you will rarely notice any important difference other than the much larger number of topics that can reasonably be supported. There are some differences in the configuration of producers and consumers, but the most critical parameters have similar meaning, and many applications use default values in any case.

If you would like to know a bit of the history of why and how MapR Streams was developed, continue with the next section. Alternatively, if you just want to know how MapR Streams works and how to use it, skip forward to "How MapR Streams Works" on page 73.

History and Context of MapR's Streaming System

The adoption of Apache Kafka for building large-scale applications over the last few years has been dramatic, and it has opened the way for support of a streaming approach. Naturally a large number of those using Kafka up to now have been technology early-adopters, which is typical in this phase of the lifecycle of an open source project. Early adopters are often able to achieve surprising levels of success very quickly with new projects like Kafka, as they have done previously with Apache projects Hadoop, Hive, Drill, Solr/Lucene, and others. These projects are groundbreaking in terms of what they make possible, and it is a natural evolution for new innovations to be implemented in emerging technology businesses before they are mature enough to be adopted by large enterprises as core technologies.

To improve the maturity of these projects, we need to solve standard questions of manageability, complexity, scalability, integration with other major technology investments, and security. In the past, with other open source projects, there have been highly variable success rates in dealing with these "enterprisey" issues. Solr, for instance, responded to security concerns by simply ruling any such concerns as out of scope, to be handled by perimeter security. The Hive community has responded to concerns about integration with SQL-generating tools by adopting Apache Calcite as a query parser and planner.

In some cases, these issues are very difficult to address within the context of the existing open source implementation. For instance, Hadoop's default file system, HDFS, supports append-only files, cannot support very many files, has had a checkered history of instability, and imposes substantial overhead because it requires use of machines that serve only to maintain metadata. Truly fixing these problems using evolutionary improvements to the existing architecture and code base would be extremely difficult. Some improvements can be made by introducing namespace federation, but while these changes may help with one problem (the limited number of files), they may exacerbate another (the amount of nonproductive overhead and instability).

If, however, a project establishes solid interface standards in the form of simple APIs early on, these problems admit a solution in the form of a complete reimplementation, possibly in open source but not necessarily. As such, Accumulo was a reimplementation of Apache HBase, incorporating features that HBase was having difficulties providing. Hypertable was another reimplementation done commercially. MapR-DB is a third reimplementation of HBase that stays close to the original HBase API as well as providing a document-style version with a JSON API.

Similarly, HDFS has seen multiple reimplementations. Some use existing storage systems, such as the S3 system of Amazon's Web Services. Others add major functionality. One example of the latter is Kosmix file system (KFS), which added mutability to files. Another example of the addition of major functionality is MapR-FS, which added full mutability, snapshotting, and higher performance and eliminated the name node issues by eliminating the name node entirely. Some reimplementations, notably Hypertable and KFS, have failed to gain significant adoption and have largely disappeared. Others, such as the S3 interface for HDFS, MapR-DB, and MapR-FS, have seen widespread adoption and use, particularly in environments very different from those that spawned HDFS in the first place. Thus, Netflix uses S3 extensively because they use Amazon's cloud infrastructure extensively, while many financial, security, and telecom applications have gravitated to MapR-FS to satisfy their

needs for stability and durability. The outcome of a reimplementation typically depends on whether or not the new project actually
solves an important problem that is difficult to change in the original project, and whether or not the original project has defined a
clean enough API to be able to be reliably implemented.

With Kafka, there are issues that look like they will turn out to be
important, and many of these appear to be difficult to resolve in the
original project. These include complexity of administration, scaling, security, and the question of how to handle multiple models of
data storage (such as files and tables), as well as data streams in a
single, converged architecture.

MapR Streams is a reimplementation of Kafka that aims to solve
these problems while keeping very close to the API that Kafka provides. Even though the interface is similar, the implementation is
very different. MapR Streams is fundamentally based on the same
MapR technology core that anchors MapR-FS and MapR-DB. This
allows MapR Streams to reuse many of the solutions already available in MapR's technology core for administration, security, disaster
protection, and scale. Interestingly, reimplementing Kafka using different technology only became possible with the Kafka 0.9 API. Earlier APIs exposed substantial amounts of internal implementation
details that made it nearly impossible to reimplement in a substantially improved way.

How MapR Streams Works

To understand how MapR Streams works internally, it is useful to
know that it operates in a completely different way than Kafka does.
Kafka's internal mechanism establishes a strong identity between
individual files and replicas of topic partitions. Messages sent to a
topic are appended to the most current file in a partition. When the
current file becomes large, a new one is opened. Thus, a producer
sending messages results in efficient sequential writes to disk at the
Kafka broker. When a consumer reads messages starting at some
offset, all that needs to happen is for a file to be opened and messages sent to the consumer using sequential reads. Both of these
processes are fast and simple. This simplicity, however, also imposes
a number of limitations on Kafka. The limitation on the number of
partitions per broker, for instance, stems directly from this implementation choice. Likewise, it is essential that a partition fit entirely

on a single file system on a single broker in order to guarantee that the request for messages from a topic partition is received by a broker (regardless of which messages). The key virtue of the sequential file I/O strategy used in Kafka, for the most part, is that batches of messages can be written and read using only relatively large sequential I/O operations on a single file.

With MapR Streams, the fundamental internal technology is quite different. Instead of basing the implementation directly on generic file capabilities, Streams explicitly uses mechanisms such as transactions, containers, and B-trees that are available inside the MapR data platform. These primitive mechanisms allow a MapR stream to model all of the necessary user-visible capabilities of the Kafka API, such as messages and producer and consumer offsets, directly in the stream object that lives in the data platform. The MapR data platform has existing segmentation techniques to distribute large objects across multiple containers and to replicate the blocks inside a container so neither of these issues has to be addressed in the stream implementation itself. Likewise, streams benefit from the way that the MapR platform can efficiently transform updates to table-like data structures into large, sequential I/O operations. Therefore, while Kafka is designed to directly implement these large transfers, MapR Streams simply inherits the property of efficient I/O patterns from the core platform. The Kafka strategy is better if there is no technology core beyond simple files; the MapR strategy allows a wide range of capabilities to be implemented very quickly, but only if the core platform is available.

Because each message is addressed individually in MapR Streams, the cost of a stream depends almost entirely on the total number of messages it contains. Whether the messages are in a single topic or in many makes almost no difference. The exception is that the total number of partitions into which messages are actively being written provides a soft bound on the degree of parallelism. This is a soft bound because automatic stream segmentation can cause the hot part of each partition to move from machine to machine very quickly, if need be, to amortize the total load over many machines. This also means that having a very large number of topics and partitions in a stream is not very expensive. The grouping of topics— even a large number of topics—into a stream for collective management is depicted in Figure 5-1. This can be useful, for example, if you are monitoring sensor data from a large number of automobiles, because you can have a topic per car to which all the measurements from that car are sent. Similarly, you could have a topic per visitor on a website. The result of this flexibility about which data goes into which topic and how many topics you have means that you can effectively sort data into sessions or device histories as it arrives. That can be very useful for certain kinds of analytics.

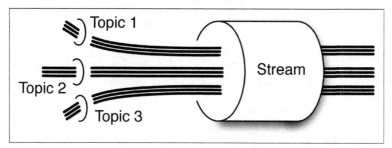

Figure 5-1. With MapR Streams, topics are grouped together into a management structure known as a stream. A MapR stream can contain an astounding number of topics—up to millions. By collecting topics together, it's convenient to apply policies such as time-to-live to the whole group of topics. Each topic in a MapR stream can be partitioned similarly to how that is done in Kafka. (See Chapter 4, Figure 4-2, for a comparison.) In the current figure, partitions are shown as thick black lines.

How to Configure MapR Streams

One important aspect in which MapR Streams differs from the Kafka 0.9 API is that there are far fewer configuration properties for Streams, and some are unique to Streams. Table 5-1 shows the important producer configuration properties and highlights those properties that are common to both Kafka and Streams, as well as the serialization properties that are common to both producer and consumer configurations.

Key among these differences is a way to set the default stream for a producer. Since Kafka has no concept comparable to a stream, MapR Streams uses the topic name to define which stream is being used. The convention is that the full path of the stream is used, followed by a slash or colon and the topic name. If the streams.pro ducer.default.stream property is set, then for all topic names that do not begin with a slash, the part of the path name up to the topic name is taken from this property instead of from the topic name.

Note that there is no `bootstrap.servers` property to help connect either producer or consumer to a cluster of brokers. This is unnecessary in programs using MapR Streams since there are no brokers to contact.

Table 5-1. Important producer configuration properties for MapR Streams. Items with an asterisk function the same as for Kafka; a double asterisk indicates a property that applies to the consumer as well as producer.

Property	Description	Default value
`buffer.memory*`	Size of producer buffer memory	33554432
`client.id*`	Producers can tag data to allow consumers to know the source	None
`key.serializer**`	The serializer used by the producer and consumer for keys	None
`value.serializer**`	The serializer used by the producer and consumer for values	
`streams.buffer.max.time.ms`	How long data is buffered by the producer before sending	3,000 ms
`streams.pro ducer.default.stream`	The name of the stream to be used for topics that do not start with /	

The configuration properties for consumers are shown in Table 5-2. Again, properties that Streams has in common with Kafka are marked with an asterisk, and again, there is no `bootstrap.servers` property since there are no brokers to contact.

On the consumer side, one interesting difference is the `streams.con sumer.buffer.memory` property. This sets the amount of data the consumer will pre-fetch from the stream. With Kafka, no data is read from a broker until the `poll()` method on the KafkaConsumer object is called. With MapR Streams, however, data is pre-fetched from subscribed topics in order to allow overlap between fetching and computing. This can drive apparent latency for reading messages to essentially zero. Read-ahead does not actually affect the end-to-end latency, however.

As with the producer API, a default stream can be set to allow simple topic names to be used.

*Table 5-2. The most important consumer properties for MapR Streams.
The properties marked with an asterisk have the same function for Apache
Kafka.*

Property	Description	Defult value
`auto.commit.inter val.ms*`	How often offsets are committed if `auto.off set.reset` is true	
`auto.offset.reset*`	One of `earliest`, `latest`, `none`, to determine where a newly created offset for a consumer group should be placed	`lat est`
`enable.auto.commit*`	Enables auto-commit of topic offsets	true
`fetch.min.bytes*`	If fewer than this number of bytes are available on the server, the request will block until this many bytes are available	1 byte
`fetch.max.wait.ms*`	How long a request will wait if it doesn't have enough bytes to return	
`group.id*`	The name of the consumer group for this consumer	
`max.parti tion.fetch.bytes*`	The amount of data that the consumer will try to fetch from the stream on each request	64 kB
`streams.con sumer.buffer.memory`	Specifies how much memory to use for pre-fetching messages	64 MB
`streams.con sumer.default.stream`	Specifies the stream to use by default for topics whose names don't start with /	

Geo-Distributed Replication

MapR Streams supports a number of data center-to-data center replication features. This type of replication goes beyond what can be
done at present with Apache Kafka's MirrorMaker function. The key
here is the use of near–real time replication technology similar to
the technology used by MapR-DB. This near–real time replication
allows continuous transfer of updated records. Interestingly, the rep-

lication graph can have loops in it without problems because records that arrive via multiple paths are detected before transmission.

Examples of replication patterns are found in Figure 5-2. Case A shows a simple bidirectional replication between two data centers. Messages can be inserted in the replicated stream in either data center and the changes will be replicated to the other data center as soon as possible. Case B shows a more complex case in which data is shared bidirectionally between San Francisco and Singapore data centers and between Singapore and Sydney data centers. Messages can be inserted into the replicated stream in any data center, although any given topic should only have messages inserted in one data center at a time. In case C, there are no replication loops. Data from New York propagates to London, as does data from Paris to London, but no data is propagated back. The time-to-live can be adjusted so data in New York and Paris only lasts a short while and data in London can be set to be retained for a long time. The ability to replicate data this way is useful for data acquisition use cases. This last case is the only one of the three that can be done easily in Kafka.

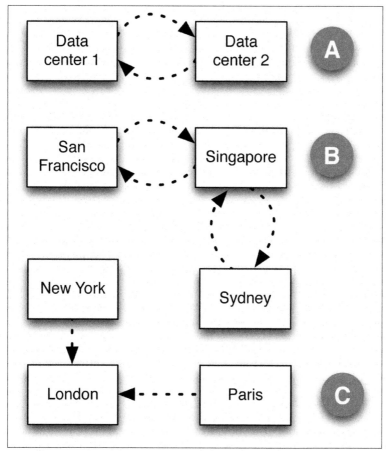

Figure 5-2. Replication of streams between clusters can have loops with MapR Streams. This is not possible using MirrorMaker with Kafka.

MapR Streams Gotchas

There are a number of issues that may affect whether or not MapR Streams is a good choice for streaming architectures in your projects. For one thing, it is relatively new, with a first GA release early in 2016. This youth isn't quite as serious at it looks, because the underlying technology has been battle-tested since 2010, but it is definitely a consideration, at least in the near term. Since Kafka's API for version 0.9 is also new but built on solid foundations, both systems share the situation of being both young and mature at the same time.

Another issue is that MapR Streams only supports the new Kafka API that was introduced in the Kafka 0.9 release. Applications based on Kafka 0.8 or earlier APIs will not be directly compatible. The conversion is very simple, but it must be done in order to use MapR Streams, so this requires some additional effort. The same effort is required for Kafka users who choose to take advantage of the improvements in Kafka's 0.9 release—they would still have to do some rewriting (modifications) to run their older Kafka applications on the new API.

One interesting difference between the two systems is that with Kafka, administrators must take on a much more active role, and in some cases must explicitly position topic partitions in the cluster. In MapR clusters, users have far less control over exactly where different topic partitions are stored and accessed. A stream can be limited to a part of a larger cluster using volume topology, but there is no equivalent of the manual positioning of data that is available in Kafka. Whether this is a virtue or a vice with MapR Streams depends very much on your application and whether low-level administration is a good or bad thing in your environment.

To use the geo-replication features of MapR Streams, you should pay attention to several factors. The first is that, while entire streams can make use of multi-master replication, individual topics in a replicated stream should only have messages inserted in a single replica. If all replicas are up to date, you can change which replica gets the messages first, but you should not insert messages into replicas in the same topic in many locations simultaneously. Typically, the way that this is handled is to either have a topic per location that is used specifically to ingest data from that location, or to change the insert point for each topic relatively slowly with respect to the replication rate.

Sample MapR Streams Programs

You can find a blog post with detailed examples on how to code for MapR Streams with a link to the associated GitHub repository containing the sample applications (*http://bit.ly/mapr-streams-code-samples*). Remember that coding for MapR Streams is based on Kafka's 0.9 API.

CHAPTER 6

Fraud Detection with Streaming Data

Rapid detection of credit card fraud is just one of many examples from the financial sector where streaming data is an important part of the solution. In this chapter, we'll show how stream-based architecture can provide a better architectural foundation for credit card fraud detection and, if designed in a clever way, also provide benefits for projects beyond the first specific goal for fraud protection.

Thinking of the example in this way, we have two major goals in our design:

Goal 1

> When a customer uses a credit card to do a transaction, the vendor needs a fast response to the question, "Is it fraud?"

Goal 2

> We need to keep a history of fraud decisions the system has made. That history of decisions should be available to other applications and services within the organization as well as updating the database within the fraud system.

Card Velocity

For our credit card example, in order to highlight the architectural aspects, we take a highly simplified view of how to actually detect fraud. Specifically, we'll look at a property known as *card velocity* and use it as an indicator of the likelihood of fraudulent activity. The idea behind card velocity is quite straightforward. Suppose you see that a credit card is used at a point of sale (POS) in London, and three minutes later, the same card is used at a POS in Sydney, Australia. What do you conclude? Until someone invents an effective molecular transporter or time machine, it's likely that one or both credit card transactions are fraudulent.

Identifying fraudulent activity sounds easy to do, and basically it is, except that these decisions have to be made for millions of transactions, and very quickly. After a decision is made about the relative likelihood of fraud for each one, the result must be returned reliably to the POS with a latency of just a few dozen milliseconds. That's where machine-based decisions and a system for handling message streams become important. Figure 6-1 shows the high-level structure of our sample system. In the figure, the decision engine used to decide whether or not a transaction appears to be fraudulent is represented by a question mark in a box; we will explain what lies within the box next. The point is that many POS terminals can send requests for decisions to the same decision engine.

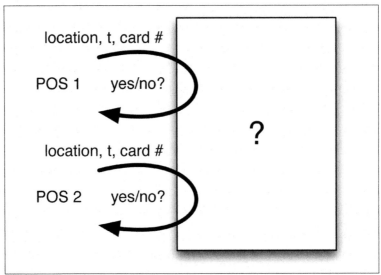

Figure 6-1. When a credit card transaction takes place, a request is sent from the POS to a data center to ask if the transaction is likely to be fraudulent (yes/no?). The request identifies the event with data that includes location and time of the transaction and the card number. This simple diagram highlights the idea that a huge number of credit card transaction requests are coming in at nearly the same time. The

decision needs to be made and the answer provided within about 50–100 milliseconds.

Keep in mind that our example is simplified for sake of illustration. Card velocity is, in fact, often used in real fraud detection systems as one indicator of credit card fraud, but it's only one of hundreds of such indicators. These systems tend to be complex and involve weighing combinations of many indicators. We are focusing on the overall architecture, however, so we will keep this example simple.

Fast Response Decision to the Question: "Is It Fraud?"

We will use card velocity as the method to detect an anomalous transaction that might signal a fraud attempt. To do that, each transaction needs to include information about the purchase location and time, as well as some way to identify it as being associated with a particular credit card, such as the card number. This information needs to be conveyed with the request to the fraud detector application at a data center for each request, as shown in Figure 6-2.

We won't go into the details of the fraud detector application here (we have discussed similar cases in other publications), but at a high level, what is involved is a system trained to recognize what represents a range for normal behavior related to the time interval between two successive transactions and the distance between locations. In our simplified example, the model only needs to retain the previous location. For building a more complex model, however, we would need to collect card transaction histories and use this data to train a more sophisticated detection model. In anticipation of that, we design the architecture such that collecting transaction histories is easy, even though we don't necessarily need to do it for the current step.

To actually make a fraud decision, we need to look up the previous use of the card and subtract that location and time of use from the data for the current transaction to compute the card velocity. We use this computation to decide if the velocity is too high to be trusted.

These steps are depicted in the architecture diagram shown in Figure 6-2.

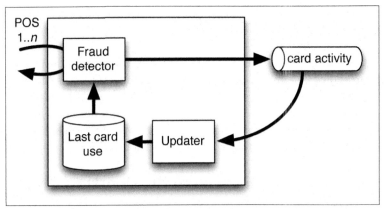

Figure 6-2. The diagram shows an architectural design for the data flow needed to meet the goal of a fast response for credit card transaction verification. The fraud detector makes a decision about card activity and returns that decision back to the POS. It also records the transaction information and decision so that an updater program can make a record of the last use. The update provides information about the last card use, which in turn will be used as reference data when the next fraud decision is made.

Notice that the POS sends a query to the fraud detector and expects a response to be returned directly. We don't implement this step using streaming because a query-response style is a more appropriate match for user expectations in this situation. However, we do publish the output of the detector, including the card and transaction information and the fraud decision, to a message stream for later processing. This stream is shown as a horizontal tube labeled "card activity" in Figure 6-2.

Publishing historical transactions to a stream is appropriate because we don't want the fraud detector to know or care how the historical transactions are used—we want to completely decouple any current or future consumers of that data from the fraud detector itself. Having a stream of transaction information available actually helps build the more complex fraud detection mechanisms that would be used in reality.

On the other hand, even in our simplified card velocity example, a database is needed to store the last transaction information so that it is easy to look up the transaction by card number. It is tempting to build this system by having the fraud detector directly update the database each time a decision is made. In practice, it is actually better to send all transactions to a message stream that is outside the fraud detector and then reimport that information into the database inside the fraud detector. This design is nonintuitive, but the rationale becomes clearer as we talk about scaling our fraud detector prototype. The database, by the way, might be built using Apache HBase or MapR's integrated NoSQL document-style database, MapR JSON DB.

The data flow shown in Figure 6-1 meets the needs of Goal 1, but by using the message stream (Kafka or MapR Streams) as in Figure 6-2, it also helps to set you up for other projects, which is our Goal 2.

Multiuse Streaming Data

Almost as soon as a system like our fraud detector prototype is built, additional requirements will be added. For instance, whoever is charged with building the next-generation model for the fraud detector will want to analyze historical data. Other projects beyond fraud detection also may need to make use of the card transaction data.

A streams-based architecture makes it possible to design a system in which you can easily add additional services. In this case, the dataflow design for fraud detection based on card velocity makes the data about card activity more widely available, as depicted in Figure 6-3. In particular, exposing the card activity message queue to other internal services makes it easy for other services to see a comprehensive view of all authorization traffic. Remember that this data stream includes the decision results output by the fraud detector.

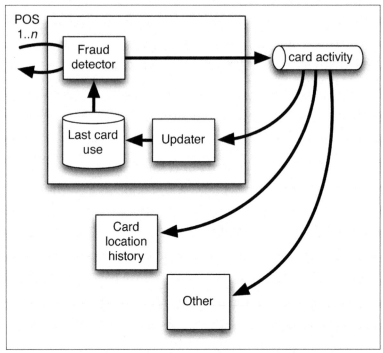

Figure 6-3. An advantage of using a message queue for the output of the fraud detector is shown here. This design lets us use the card activity and fraud decision data more broadly. Having a long retention time for data in the queue is also very useful. For example, that data could be queried by a process to build a collection of card location histories stored in a data format such as Parquet that allows very efficient querying. Other processes might use data from the card activity queue to determine the rate of fraud among subscribers or to build a real-time display of where transactions are happening.

Scaling Up the Fraud Detector

We just saw how a streaming architecture allows us to build a simple fraud detection prototype that also allows other services to access data so that historical analyses can improve the decision model or so that real-time displays can show us what is happening in the moment.

A streaming architecture helps in other ways as well. Figure 6-4 shows how multiple fraud detectors can use the same card activity message queue.

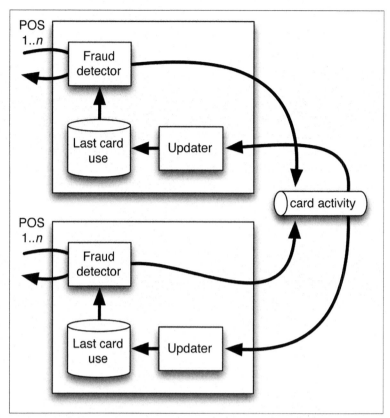

Figure 6-4. Multiple fraud detectors can use the same message queue. This design enables each of them to use all of the card activity data and thus be able to handle any incoming transaction.

The idea is that since all fraud models send all of their transactions to the card activity message queue, that queue will have a complete view of all card activity. Each instance of the fraud detector will not depend on any of the other instances, except insofar as more data will appear in each local database. The decoupling between services inherent in the streaming design allows the fraud service to be scaled relatively easily. Similarly, because each instance of the fraud detector maintains its own database of last card usage locations, new instances can be fielded that use alternative kinds of databases. If the number of transactions per second grows high enough that the current version of the detector cannot handle it, then an in-memory database can be fitted instead. Alternatively, the card activity message queue can use a partitioned topic so each fraud detector can be designed to handle only one partition.

Summary

In this fraud detection example, we've seen how the use of a message stream can make data available to more than one service without creating dependencies. In this way, the universal streaming-first design provides a powerful and flexible system that supports the microservices approach. For best results, it should become a habit in how you think about architectures that best suit your purposes.

CHAPTER 7
Geo-Distributed Data Streams

For our final example of how to design stream-based systems, we focus on a specific requirement: geo-distributed replication of data streams. This capability is needed in a wide variety of sectors, including telecommunications, oil and gas exploration, retail, and banking, but we've chosen a transportation example—international container shipping—to show you how to plan the data flow for systems that require data to be replicated efficiently across distant locations.

For this example, we focus on how the design would work with MapR Streams because it has special capabilities that make it particularly well suited for this class of use cases. MapR Streams is distinctive in being able to:

- Handle huge numbers of topics (hundreds of thousands or more with high throughput)
- Organize a group of topics into a stream, which makes data management much easier since many topics can be managed together
- Provide uni- and bi-directional replication easily and reliably across geo-distributed data centers

In our shipping example (or examples from any of the other sectors), many different processes in addition to the messaging could be taking place on the same cluster since MapR's messaging feature is integrated into the data platform. But for simplicity and in order to keep our explanation focused on how the data streams are replicated to distant sites, we will just examine the messaging aspect of the architecture rather than all the analytics and persistence components.

As we work through this IoT transportation example, envision how this type of design would play out in your own projects. You may not have ships and containers, but you may well have data needs that are similar.

Stakeholders

Let's set the scene: in international container shipping, different stakeholders are interested in using shipping data in different ways. How you would choose to organize data depends on the interest of each stakeholder. What data would be assigned to separate topics? How many topics? Which topics would be grouped together into streams? When would you use geo-distributed stream replication?

There is no single correct design for this container shipping example, but by exploring the implications of a particular set of design choices, you can better decide how you would assign data to topics and streams in your own examples.

In our hypothetical example, here are the players: we have a fictional giant shipping company, Big Blue, that owns a fleet of ships and hundreds of thousands of shipping containers. Big Blue is based out of Los Angeles, but its ships travel to ports all around the world, including Tokyo, Sydney, and Singapore; the latter city is shown in Figure 7-1. Big Blue not only ships cargo in its own containers, but it also leases space for containers owned by other shipping companies or by large manufacturers. Big Blue wants to know where its ships are, which containers have arrived at what ports, and what the environmental conditions are like on board and on shore. Branch offices of Big Blue are located in major ports, and they want to be able to share data among themselves as well as to report back to Big Blue's headquarters.

Figure 7-1. Singapore is shown here at night. A large portion of the world's container shipping passes through this port, where huge stacks of containers are monitored via sensor data while they are being loaded onto and off of ships.

Who else is interested in the shipping-related data? Another major group of stakeholders are manufacturers who are paying to ship goods with Big Blue. Back at their corporate headquarters, the manufacturers want to know the status of their goods in terms of what environmental conditions they are being exposed to during their voyage and during transfers as well as to track the progress of these goods to their destination. The recipients of the goods who've paid to purchase them also want this information, although perhaps in a less fine-grained manner. Port authorities at each stop have their own interests. They are not just interested in the ships and containers of Big Blue but rather in knowing exactly which ships of various companies have docked or departed, what containers have been delivered to the docks to be loaded, or what has been unloaded. These are just some of the major players.

Design Goals

Now that we've considered the interests of some of the major stakeholders, we can put together a short list of design goals. Again, we have greatly simplified this example so that we can more easily follow the geo-distribution aspect of data and how the messaging layer supports data flow in this design. Here are some of the things our design must do:

- Reliably ingest, analyze, and retain very large-volume data from continuous events and measurements (including IoT sensor data) with high performance and low latency
- Decouple consolidation and processing steps at data centers from delivery of data from sources such as sensors
- Control access by easily managing who can see what data
- Cope with intermittent transmission of ship-to-shore data while the ship is at sea
- Efficiently replicate data streams across geo-distributed clusters, including between ports, from port to manufacturing or shipping headquarters, and from ship to shore

Design Choices

With these goals as a guide, we can begin to make design choices. For the simplified scope of our explanation, we'll follow the data involved in shipping some plastic duck toys from their origin in Tokyo. The headquarters for the manufacturer is also located in Tokyo, and the company engages Big Blue Shipping to transport the toy ducks, as illustrated in Figure 7-2. To demonstrate our design choices, we'll follow data as a ship arrives in Tokyo (A), takes on a load of toy ducks and other goods, then heads for Singapore (B). Some of the containers of ducks are off-loaded in Singapore, where a few will go to local retail outlets and the rest will await transfer to another ship to be taken to London (not shown on our diagram). The rest of the duck-filled containers will continue on the original ship to the port of Sydney (C) along with new containers owned by other companies that were loaded on in Singapore.

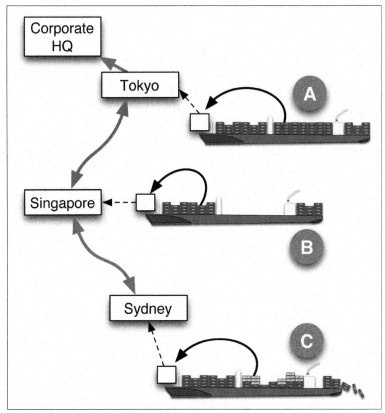

Figure 7-2. The diagram shows data flow for a container shipping company. Data from environmental sensors and tracking sensors on the containers is continuously streamed (black arrows) to an onboard cluster (white square) owned by the shipping company. When the ship arrives in a port, a temporary connection is made (dashed arrow) to stream data from the onboard cluster to an onshore data center cluster (not shown) owned by the shipping company. Streams are also replicated bidirectionally between data centers in different ports (double-headed gray arrows).

Our Design

Big Blue has equipped each of its ships with a small data cluster and a cell network. The onboard cluster continuously collects IoT data from sensors on the various containers as well as some sensors located on the ship itself. Each port also has a data center cluster that belongs to Big Blue. When a ship arrives near a port, it establishes a temporary connection and streams data from its onboard cluster to the cluster onshore at the port.

In our design, we assign a topic to each container (one ship can have up to tens of thousands of containers and therefore as many topics). These per-container topics are managed by putting them into a single stream that is replicated worldwide to all Big Blue facilities. In addition, because Big Blue is also interested in the travel history for each of its ships, we assign each ship a topic and manage these using a single, worldwide Big Blue ships stream. The per-ship topics serve much like an old-fashioned ship's log. Ship-specific data could be contained in more than one ship-related topic; perhaps data for the ship's location goes to one topic for that ship while environmental sensor data for the ship goes to another topic, and all are organized into the ships stream along with topics from other ships in the Big Blue fleet.

Follow the Data

What are the implications of this design relative to our design goals and the stakeholder's needs? We'll look at just a part of the system, with reference to Figure 7-2. Starting at stage A, our ship has been loaded in Tokyo, and its onboard cluster provides updates to the Tokyo Big Blue cluster with data about the ship (two topics in the ships stream) and about which containers have been loaded onto the ship, some with ducks and some with other goods (one topic per container; updates to thousands of topics in the containers stream). The Tokyo Big Blue cluster reports a subset of this information to the headquarters of the toy manufacturing company (labeled Corporate HQ in Figure 7-2). These updates are also propagated in near–real time to data centers in other ports and to Big Blue headquarters.

As the ship heads for Singapore, sensors on board continue to send messages to topics in the streams on the ship's cluster. The ship does not normally communicate large amounts of data directly with any of the onshore clusters since satellite data transmission is so expensive. However, when the ship arrives in Singapore, container topics on the Singapore Big Blue cluster have already been updated about which containers were loaded in Tokyo. This was done directly between the Tokyo and Singapore clusters via the geo-distributed streams replication capability of MapR Streams. When the ship arrives in port, it establishes a temporary connection with the Singapore cluster and further updates it with event data collected during the passage from the containers and the ship itself. The geo-distributed streams replication is bidirectional, so this new information is copied back to Tokyo as well as on ahead to Sydney.

Some containers are offloaded in Singapore and new ones owned by someone other than Big Blue (depicted by a different color in our figure) are loaded on board. Sensors report which containers were left behind and which new ones were loaded on (updates to their topics for the containers stream or a new topic if the container is newly placed in service). Sensor data also confirms that the remainder of the containers are still safely on board.

Control Who Has Access to Stream Data

Here's another aspect of how our design meets the design goals. The owners of the new containers may want access to the message data related to their containers, but Big Blue does not want them to have access to all of the data. Fortunately, MapR Streams enables fine-grained control over who has access to data. Access Control Expressions (ACEs) are assigned at the Streams level, so you could set up a separate stream for the yellow and red container topics. That way Big Blue provides a customer with access to topics related to their own containers while restricting data access to Big Blue streaming data.

Back to our ship: next, the ship heads for Sydney. As before, data reaches the next port before the ship does. Data that the ship uploaded to the onshore Singapore cluster will reach the Sydney cluster via MapR Streams replication. This replication is triggered by the updates to topics that took place in Singapore. When the ship arrives in Sydney, a temporary ship-to-shore connection once again is established, and data for events during the passage is delivered to the Sydney cluster.

While the ship is in port, sensors on containers continue to provide a flow of data to the onboard cluster to report their status as some containers are offloaded and some remain on board. This message flow from sensors is how the onboard cluster receives the information that triggers an alert when several containers of toy ducks slip off the back of the ship (stage C in Figure 7-2). This information will be replicated in seconds to the port clusters as well as back to Big Blue headquarters in Los Angeles. The managers will not be happy when they have to send a report to the toy manufacturer to tell them the fate of the lost toy ducks (check your local beaches to see where they end up.)[1]

Advantages of Streams-based Geo-Replication

In our "toy example" (pun intended) architecture, our use of a topic per container and topics grouped as a container stream means that the topic provides a continuous history of that particular container, even through its life on different ships or on docks in different ports. The organization into a stream is convenient because time-to-live, geo-distributed replication, and data access control can all be set at the stream level.

The huge number of containers to be tracked by an international shipping company would require the ability to handle up to hundreds of thousands of topics per stream or more. At present, MapR Streams is unusual among messaging technologies in its ability to handle that number of topics. The MapR Streams capability for multi-master geo-distributed replication is also distinctive and beneficial. We chose this particular example because it brings the issues of huge numbers of topics, intermittent network connections, streaming client fail-over, and geo-distribution into the foreground, but these issues exist in many situations without being quite so obvious.

---

1 Our example is a nod to a real event in which toy ducks, turtles, beavers, and frogs, called "Friendly Floatees," were lost at sea in the Pacific off a ship that sailed from Hong Kong in 1992. Some arrived in Alaska in late 1992. Most recent Floatee sightings were on UK beaches in 2007. For more information, see *https://bit.ly/lost-ducks*.

CHAPTER 8

Putting It All Together

Where do you go from here?

Try reexamining your goals for different projects and see what advantages you might gain from transitioning to a universal stream-based approach in addition to the specific benefits for your real-time analytics applications.

The fact is, there's a revolution in what you can do with streaming data for a wide variety of use cases, from IoT sensor data to financial services, telecommunications, web-based business, retail, healthcare, and more. New technologies that efficiently handle continuous event data with speed at scale are part of why this revolution is possible. Another key ingredient is a new way to design architecture that exploits these emerging technologies. The big change is to see the power in a universal stream-based design. This does not mean that streaming data is used for everything, but it does mean that streaming becomes a common approach rather than something considered only for specialized, real-time projects.

 There are great benefits to be gained when stream-based designs for big data architectures become a habit.

At the heart of effective stream-based architecture is the message passing itself. A big difference between stream-based and traditional design (or even people's preconception of streaming) is that the messaging layer plays a much more prominent role. It can and should be used for more than just a step to precede real-time analytics, although it is essential for processing streaming data in these applications. For this type of messaging to be effective, it needs to be a Kafka-esque style tool. New technologies continue to be developed, but at present we see Apache Kafka and MapR Streams as good choices for the messaging layer to support the capabilities needed for an effective stream-based system. Whatever stream messaging technology you choose, you should ask if it has the following essential capabilities.

Key Qualities of Messaging Technology

To get the real benefits of streaming architecture, a messaging technology needs to have the following characteristics:

- Replayable
- Persistent
- Capable of high performance at large scale

For the processing components of modern streaming architectures, there are a variety of strong technologies. We see particular promise with Apache Spark Streaming and with Apache Flink projects, each of which takes a somewhat different approach. Spark Streaming is an additional feature of the widely popular Spark software. It takes advantage of in-memory processing for speed and uses a special case of batch processing—microbatches—to approximate real-time analytics. Flink is a new technology that also provides speed at scale but approaches streaming from the side of real-time stream processing that can be cut into batch processing as necessary. Both systems are very attractive options to complement the messaging layer.

Benefits of Stream-based Architectures

One of the benefits of adopting a stream-based architecture with effective messaging is that it gives you a system that is faster due to less data motion. This approach is convenient: there is less administration needed and fewer moving parts to coordinate. It's a powerful way to support microservices that in turn make your organization more agile. A messaging component used in the right places in an architectural design serves to decouple services; the source of data does not have to coordinate with the consumer. That's also why persistence matters for messages: if the consumer is not available when the message is delivered, that's OK—it will be available when it is needed. It's not that a query-and-response approach is never useful; it's just that the stream-based messaging layer can be powerful in many parts of the design.

Another aspect of these designs and the desire for flexibility is to provide data that multiple consumers will use in different ways. That underlines the importance of delivering and persisting raw data in many situations, because at the time you design an architecture and data flow, you may not know all the applications for which you may need this data or indeed what aspects of the data will ultimately be important.

Effective handling of streaming data lets you more easily respond to changing events and react to life as it happens by acting on real-time insights.

Geo-distributed replication of data streams greatly expands the impact of stream-based architectures. We provided an example use case in Chapter 7, but the advantages of being able to rapidly share streaming data across multiple data centers applies to use cases in many sectors. At present, MapR Streams is the messaging technology that best fits these capabilities.

Making the Transition to Streaming Architecture

As you plan new projects, building your design based on a streaming architecture becomes fairly straightforward, and that in turn gives you greater flexibility for future modifications. But how do you incorporate the stream-based style of architecture when you have legacy services?

The good news is that it is easier to migrate to messaging-style applications than you might think. The flexibility imparted by a broader role for messaging also gives you an effective and relatively convenient way to incorporate change into your legacy projects. Here's how it works.

One of the limitations of traditional architectures is that even if they work efficiently on those jobs for which they were originally designed, when you try to add a service or make a modification, change is difficult. This is true, in part, because of strong dependencies between services, as suggested by the diagram in Figure 8-1.

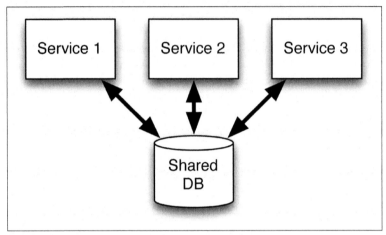

Figure 8-1. Traditional architecture in which components are strongly coupled is shown in this figure. In this design, Services 1, 2, and 3 use data stored in a shared database and provide updates directly to the database. That may be an efficient arrangement, but if you try to modify any of these services, the dependencies result in unwanted changes to the entire system.

Suppose you want to make a change to one of your legacy services. The coupling of components in the traditional design means that the changes you make in Service 1 may also affect Services 2 and 3. The potential for such change means that the teams supporting the affected services need to be involved in the design decisions for Service 1. That can lead to bureaucratic deadlock. But you can be free to make this modification if you insert a messaging queue between the services and the database, as shown in Figure 8-2.

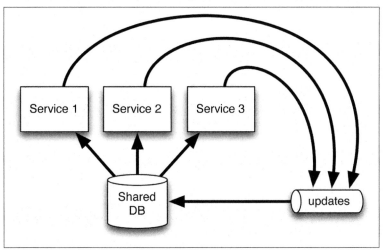

Figure 8-2. A new design for a legacy system uses a stream-based architectural approach that puts a message stream for updates between the services and the shared database. Updates from any of the services go to the stream and are subsequently reflected in the database.

The addition of the messaging layer for updates allows you to make modifications to a service without having an unwanted impact on the others. Here, all updates from Services 1–3 go through the intermediate step of a message queue, shown in Figure 8-2 as a tube labeled "updates," before reaching the shared database. Services 1–3 act as producers, and the shared database becomes a consumer of the message queue. This intermediate component decouples the producers and consumers of the data.

When you are ready to modify Service 1, you first make a copy of the database that will not be shared, as depicted in Figure 8-3. Instead, Service 1 will read from this database while Service 2 and Service 3 will continue to read from the shared database. Note that all the updates still go to the same message queue, but now the unshared database becomes a second consumer of the data. This in effect isolates the legacy services from the impact of modifications to Service 1.

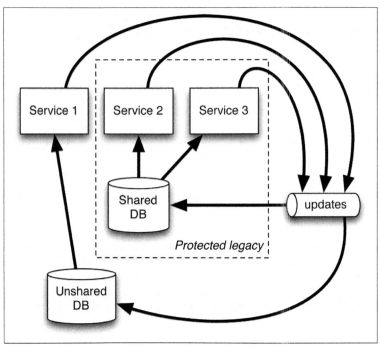

Figure 8-3. Changes are easier to make in a stream-based architecture because components are decoupled. Here, the addition of a copy of the database makes it possible to isolate the legacy services and the shared database from a newly modified Service 1. All three update the same message stream, but the legacy services can subscribe to a subset of the updates, while Service 1 can subscribe to all of them if desired. This decouples the impact of modifications to Service 1 from the legacy parts of the system.

This example is an extreme simplification to help you see how decoupling can allow you to make the transition from a traditional system to this new streaming architecture in stages. In practice, there are likely to be some issues that come up during the decoupling. One of the most serious is a dependency on transactional updates to the database. In some cases, such transactional updates can be isolated to a single service or some services may treat the database as a pure consumer, thus making the decoupling very easy. Another strategy that may be useful is to send high-level descriptions of the transaction into the message queue rather than just the low-level updates to the database tables. Sending high-level updates helps abstract the system away from the details of the database and is therefore recommended in any case.

The prospect of some difficulties should not dissuade you, however. This same basic process has been used by substantial companies in order to move legacy systems into microservices architectures.

Conclusion

With this new stream-based approach to designing architecture for big data systems, you gain greater control over who uses data and how you can build new parts of your system as you go forward. You also join the flood of people who are beginning to take advantage of streaming data with all its benefits.

> "Overall, streaming technology enables the obvious: continuous processing on data that is naturally produced by continuous real-world sources (which is most "big" data sets)."[1]
>
> —Fabian Hueske and Kostas Tzoumas, Committers
> and PMC members of Apache Flink

Most of the time, streaming data is just a better fit for how life happens.

---

1 *http://bit.ly/guide-stream-processing-flink*

Additional Resources

Streaming Data Topics

The following links and recommendations may be helpful in finding out more about streaming design and the technologies that support it:

Apache Kafka
- Project website (*http://kafka.apache.org/*)
- "Getting Started with Sample Programs for Kafka 0.9" blog (*https://www.mapr.com/blog/getting-started-sample-programs-apache-kafka-09*)

MapR Streams
- "Life of a Message in MapR Streams" blog (*http://bit.ly/mapr-streams-message*)
- MapR Streams documentation (*http://bit.ly/mapr-streams-doc*)
- "Getting Started with Sample Programs for MapR Streams" blog (*https://www.mapr.com/blog/getting-started-sample-programs-mapr-streams*)

I Heart Logs (http://bit.ly/i_heart_logs)
Book by Jay Kreps, committer and PMC member, Apache Kafka (O'Reilly).

Apache Spark Streaming
Project website (*http://spark.apache.org/streaming/*)

Getting Started with Apache Spark
Free interactive eBook by Jim Scott available for download from
MapR (*https://www.mapr.com/getting-started-apache-spark*).

Apache Flink
Project website (*https://flink.apache.org/*)

"Essential Guide to Streaming-first Processing with Apache Flink"
Blog post (*http://bit.ly/guide-stream-processing-flink*) by Fabian
Hueske and Kostas Tzoumas, committers and PMC members,
Apache Flink.

Apache Storm
Project website (*http://storm.apache.org/*)

Apache Apex
Project website (*http://apex.incubator.apache.org/*)

*University of Sheffield Advanced Manufacturing Research Centre with
Boeing including Factory 2050*
Website (*http://www.amrc.co.uk/*)

Selected O'Reilly Publications by the Authors

Short books on a variety of big data topics you may find interesting:

- *Practical Machine Learning: Innovations in Recommendation*
  (February 2014): *http://oreil.ly/1qt7riC*

- *Practical Machine Learning: A New Look at Anomaly Detection*
  (June 2014): *http://bit.ly/anomaly_detection*

- *Time Series Databases: New Ways to Store and Access Data*
  (October 2014): *http://oreil.ly/1ulZnOf*

- *Real-World Hadoop* (March 2015): *http://oreil.ly/1U4U2fN*

- *Sharing Big Data Safely: Managing Data Security* (September
  2015): *http://oreil.ly/1L5XDGv*

About the Authors

Ted Dunning is Chief Applications Architect at MapR Technologies and active in the open source community.

He currently serves as VP for Incubator at the Apache Foundation, as a champion and mentor for a large number of projects, and as committer and PMC member of the Apache ZooKeeper and Drill projects. He developed the t-digest algorithm used to estimate extreme quantiles. T-digest has been adopted by several open source projects. He also developed the open source log-synth project described in the book *Sharing Big Data Safely* (O'Reilly).

Ted was the chief architect behind the MusicMatch (now Yahoo Music) and Veoh recommendation systems, built fraud-detection systems for ID Analytics (LifeLock), and has issued 24 patents to date. Ted has a PhD in computing science from University of Sheffield. When he's not doing data science, he plays guitar and mandolin. Ted is on Twitter as *@ted_dunning*.

Ellen Friedman is a solutions consultant and well-known speaker and author, currently writing mainly about big data topics. She is a committer for the Apache Drill and Apache Mahout projects. With a PhD in Biochemistry, she has years of experience as a research scientist and has written about a variety of technical topics, including molecular biology, nontraditional inheritance, and oceanography. Ellen is also coauthor of a book of magic-themed cartoons, *A Rabbit Under the Hat* (The Edition House). Ellen is on Twitter as *@Ellen_Friedman*.

Get even more for your money.

Join the O'Reilly Community, and register the O'Reilly books you own. It's free, and you'll get:

- $4.99 ebook upgrade offer
- 40% upgrade offer on O'Reilly print books
- Membership discounts on books and events
- Free lifetime updates to ebooks and videos
- Multiple ebook formats, DRM FREE
- Participation in the O'Reilly community
- Newsletters
- Account management
- 100% Satisfaction Guarantee

Signing up is easy:

1. Go to: oreilly.com/go/register
2. Create an O'Reilly login.
3. Provide your address.
4. Register your books.

Note: English-language books only

To order books online:
oreilly.com/store

For questions about products or an order:
orders@oreilly.com

To sign up to get topic-specific email announcements and/or news about upcoming books, conferences, special offers, and new technologies:
elists@oreilly.com

For technical questions about book content:
booktech@oreilly.com

To submit new book proposals to our editors:
proposals@oreilly.com

O'Reilly books are available in multiple DRM-free ebook formats. For more information:
oreilly.com/ebooks

O'REILLY®

Have it your way.